Book of
Remembrance

Published in 2015 by 30° SOUTH PUBLISHERS (PTY) LTD.

16 Ivy Road , Pinetown 3610, South Africa

Copyright © Gerry van Tonder, 2015

Designed & typeset by SA Publishing Services (kerrincocks@gmail.com)

Cover design by Kerrin Cocks

Printed by Pinetown Printers (Pty) Ltd, Pinetown, KwaZulu-Natal

ISBN: 978-1-928211-73-0

Book of Remembrance

Rhodesia Native Regiment & Rhodesian African Rifles

Gerry van Tonder

Commissioned by the RAR Regimental Association (UK)

Memorial Donors

The Memorial in the National Memorial Arboretum is intended to stand in eternal recognition of the fellowship, skill, bravery and sacrifice for which these regiments are renowned and it is poignant that it has been erected in the centenary years of World War One.

The publication of this book and the construction of the memorial, to which it relates, have been made possible by the generous and whole-hearted support of numerous benefactors. Contributions, both great and small, have been made with love and respect, to commemorate those who served as soldiers of the Regiments and especially those who made the supreme sacrifice in the service of freedom and humanity. Without these generous donations, many of which were anonymous, it would not have been possible to recognise and celebrate these proud regiments and the courage and achievements of the men who mustered to the call of duty under their colours.

All donations, of whatever amount, have been gratefully received and are respectfully acknowledged, especially from those whose family members are commemorated herein.

Memorial stones have been dedicated to:

- L.Cpl. Adam, Pte. Madzivanyika, Pte. Fanuwel Nharo. "In memory of three brave 1RAR soldiers who lost their lives on 5th April 1972, from Ian Robertson."
- Brave men, "Who continue to make us proud of our Motherland, from T.M. Johnson."
- Major-General R.E.B. Long. "From David Long."
- Major D.E. (Taffy) Marchant. "In memory of my uncle, from Mike Moran."
- Sgt. George Mleya 1RAR "Killed in action 21st. February 1979. A fine soldier of Rhodesia – respectfully remembered, from Jim Galloway."

- L.Cpl. T.J. Murdock. "In memory of a brilliant son of truly blessed parents, Jill and Brian Murdock and a wonderful brother of Julia."
- Lt. Ian Wardle BCR. "In memory of my dear brave father who was awarded the Bronze Cross of Rhodesia for his bravery. Sadly he died when I was five but I never forget him. With love from your son, Angus Joseph Wardle."
- Rhodesian African Rifles. "Remembered with gratitude and pride, from Ian and Shirley Findlay (Internal Affairs)."
- Lt. N.J. Smith 1RAR. "Killed in action 22nd. August 1967. In memory of my brother, from Mrs. Cherry Bessant."

Memorial stones have been donated by:

- John Anderson
- N.I.F. (Norman) Baker
- Beit Trust
- Captain A. Bent
- Lieutenant-Colonel M.L. Clewer
- Bill and Judy Cochrane
- Mrs. Jenny Daines
- Red de Vries
- On behalf of Lieutenant-Colonel Billy Conn by Judy Donner.
- Ann Fairs and family
- Lieutenant-Colonel D.P. Hobson
- Dr. Jon Howat
- Colyn James (RhAF)
- Captain Trevor Jones
- Peter Kerruish (Royal Welsh)
- Brigadier Pat Lawless
- The Leonard family

- Brian Lennon-Smith and family
- Rory McKenna
- Ron Marillier
- Rob Merrifield
- Mike Moran
- Ann and Dick Paget
- Athol (Jock) Pirie
- Captain A.J. Reyneke
- Michael Roberts
- Bruce Robinson
- Mrs. Nicki Salt
- Mrs. June Shaw-Violet
- Major-General Mike Shute OLM and family
- Brigadier Ian Stansfield
- Major Wayne Thompson
- Douglas Veremu
- Major J.R. (Buttons) Wells-West
- Ray Wilson
- Captain John Wynne-Hopkins

The fundraising committee thank all who have made this memorial possible.

Contents

The Author

Gerry van Tonder was born in Bulawayo, Rhodesia. After attending Hamilton High in that city, he completed his secondary education at Thornhill High in Gwelo.

He joined Internal Affairs in January 1975, and was stationed at Karoi, as a Cadet District Officer. A year later, he reported to Chikurubi in Salisbury as a member of Internal Affairs National Service 4 call-up, to undergo military training. He was then posted to Sipolilo, where he was based at Fort Harrison on the Angwa River in the Zambezi Valley.

In November 1976, he was transferred to Mount Darwin, where he served in that station's intelligence section. In January 1977, he undertook the Ministry of Internal Affairs' sponsored university degree programme, graduating at the end of 1979 with a Bachelor of Administration (Honours) degree. During university vacations, he was stationed in Sipolilo and Gwelo. At the end of his studies, he was posted to Mount Darwin as a District Officer, being the Returning Officer for Rushinga during the Zimbabwe elections, and working through the period of transition from the ceasefire and return of the ZANLA insurgents to assembly points in the district.

In the middle of 1980, and with no future prospects as a civil servant, Gerry left Intaf and joined a commercial marketing firm in Salisbury. In 1983, he was headhunted by FAVCO, the country's largest fresh produce marketing cooperative, where he became managing director.

Late 1999 saw Gerry with his British-born wife Tracey leaving Zimbabwe to settle in Derby, England. Gerry has two children; a son, Andries who is currently reading for a DPhil (PhD) in Clinical Medicine (Genetics) at the University of Oxford, and a daughter, Ashleigh, a doctor who is now undergoing specialist training in gynaecology and obstetrics.

Gerry is an active member of several international networked Rhodesian associations, including the Rhodesian African Rifles Regimental Association Rhodesian Army Association (UK), the Rhodesian Services Association (New Zealand), the British South Africa Police Association (UK)and the Rhodesia Light Infantry Regimental Association (UK); the latter as a result of all three of his brothers having served in that battalion.

Gerry spends all his available spare time researching Rhodesian military history. He has co-authored *Rhodesian Combined Forces Roll of Honour 1966-1981*, *Rhodesia Regiment 1899–1981* and *Operation Lighthouse Intaf: Para-Military Civilians in Rhodesia's Bush War*. Gerry has a column in the monthly Rhodesian Service Association newsletter, *Contact! Contact!*, and is the administrator of the Face Book memorial page to Rhodesian armed forces, The Fallen. He has his own website, http://www.rhodesiansoldier.com

Acknowledgements

Brigadier David Heppenstall, after the initial approach, has been a stalwart throughout the production of this book, thank you.

My special thanks, as always, to my partner in so many Rhodesian projects big and small, Colonel Dudley Wall, former Intaf colleague, fellow author and friend. Dudley's particular talent lies with the graphics, diagrams and drawings, which he unhesitatingly produces when called upon to do so. His loyalty to the Rhodesian story remains unfaltering and total.

Particular thanks to another partner in the Rhodesian military story, Adrian Haggett. Five years on, we continue to work on the *Rhodesian Combined Forces Roll of Honour 1966–1981*. This has been an invaluable source for the upgraded, expanded and amended Bush War Rolls of Honour for the Rhodesian African Rifles found in this book. The assistance with photographic material has been invaluable, so thanks to Ralph McLean of the South Africa War Graves Project, Richard Perry, Craig Fourie, Peter Silk and Tony Beck.

Thanks to John Wynne-Hopkins for the use of his excellent paintings of the uniforms.

I acknowledge with grateful thanks, Hugh Bomford for the photo of his great-grandfather's, Lieutenant John Manners-Smith's Victoria Cross. Full recognition must be accorded the Commonwealth War Graves Commission (CWGC), whose comprehensive websites have provided invaluable information on those of the RNR and RAR who died during the two World Wars, significantly expanding our knowledge about how they died and where they have been laid to rest.

Many have contributed to the abridged histories of the various units. This compilation proved to be difficult in places as memories of a bush war that ended more than thirty years ago fade. Fortunately, a fair amount of literature exists covering the RNR, duly acknowledged in the bibliography. Thank you to Brigadier David Heppenstall for tackling this one.

The task for abridged histories of the RAR Battalions and Independent Companies proved far more onerous, particularly for the 2nd and 3rd Battalions and the Independent Companies. David Heppenstall did much to probe his networks to retrieve information from fellow officers. Peter Hosking submitted an account of 2RAR, based on an outline kindly provided by Ian Pullar. John Pritchard looked at the material, contributing names and detail where he could, but as he says, 1RAR maintained good records, but 2RAR (tongue in cheek) was too busy " getting on with the war." Alan Thrush came up with additional names of company commanding officers. Andrew Barratt provided useful accounts of Independent Company events.

My personal thanks go to General Mike Shute for his unfailing support during the project.

Foreword

The RAR Regimental Association decided to build a Memorial to the Rhodesian Native Regiment and their successors ,the Rhodesian African Rifles, in 2011. Due to the excellent support by Jennifer Upton and many others this Memorial is due to be unveiled and consecrated on Sunday 19 July 2015 at the National Memorial Arboretum at Alrewas in Staffordshire. Our Association has already planted an oak tree here to commemorate the fallen of of both of our Regiments.

Having purchased the Rhodesian Combined Forces Roll of Honour 1966-1981 by Adrian Haggett and Gerry van Tonder, I decided that it would be an excellent idea to have a similar record for the RNR and the RAR. As Gerry van Tonder was resident in the UK , he would be an ideal choice to be the author of our Book of Remembrance. Having been a District Officer with Internal Affairs during the bush war, his knowledge of African names, folklore and an attention to detail were great assets. When I approached him he agreed to be our author, commissioned by the RAR Regimental Association.

He pointed out to me, that as the name suggests, our Book of Remembrance is a written memorial to all those who sacrificed their lives in the service of the Rhodesian Native Regiment and its successor the Rhodesian African Rifles.

Apart from the *Rhodesian Combined Forces Roll of Honour 1966–1981*, Gerry has also been co-author of *Rhodesia Regiment 1899–1981*, and *Operation Lighthouse*, the Intaf story in the bush war. We thanked him for accepting the challenge.

During my twenty eight years service in the Rhodesian Army from 1952 to 1980, I served exactly half with 1RAR, including commanding officer. I enjoyed every minute of it, and am eternally proud of this fine regiment.

The Rhodesia Native Regiment began recruiting in May 1916 and deployed to German East Africa within three months. For their prowess on the battlefield, the inexperienced young soldiers earned the praise of their divisional commander. The distances they covered in three years in central and east Africa was phenomenal. Both 1RNR and 2RNR received the battle honours, The Great War and 'East Africa 1916–18'.

The successor to the RNR in World War II was the Rhodesian African Rifles, which was formed in July 1940. After three years' hard training, 1RAR was deployed to Burma, where the men again acquitted themselves very well, fighting their way down Burma, through the Arakan and Taungup areas.

After the war, 1RAR was awarded the battle honours, 'Burma 1944–45', 'Arakan Beaches' and 'Taungup'. Then three full companies and a battalion headquarters were sent to the Canal Zone, Egypt, in 1952.

On 12 July 1953, Her Majesty Queen Elizabeth, the Queen Mother, presented the Queen's Colours to the regiment on the parade ground at Borrowdale Barracks

In 1954, lRAR moved to Methuen Camp, just outside Bulawayo, where they began extensive training prior to their deployment to Malaya on anti-terrorist operations in 1956.

This was a two-year deployment, mainly in the deep jungle alongside Gurkha battalions. Three African members won the Military Medal for bravery in action.

After their return from Malaya, the battalion took part in the Nyasaland emergency in 1959 and border control on the Northern Rhodesia-Katanga border in 1961.

The government declared Unilateral Declaration of Independence on 11 November 1965, and lRAR was committed to border control duties along the Zambian border.

As the guerrilla war intensified, the men of the regiment once again proved themselves to be combatants of the first order, especially as crack airborne Fire Force troops.

The government later agreed to the formation of 2RAR in Fort Victoria and Depot RAR at Balla Balla, and in 1978, the six independent companies, which, up to then, had been staffed by white Rhodesians, were changed from Rhodesian Regiment to Rhodesian African Rifles as their numbers increasingly included more African national servicemen and regulars.

In 1979, approval was given for 3, 5 and 6 (Independent) Companies, RAR, to be regrouped and renamed 3RAR and stationed at Umtali.

The Zimbabwe elections in February-March 1980 brought Robert Mugabe to power but, initially, little was done to integrate the three erstwhile opposing forces. There was a simmering feud between ZANU and ZAPU that erupted in Bulawayo and elsewhere in 1981, which once again saw 1RAR, or 11 Infantry Battalion, as it was now called, in action. The Battle for Bulawayo, as it became known, was a magnificent finale to lRAR's history, and indeed the regiment's swansong.

Our soldiers of all ranks, black and white, were a pleasure with whom to serve. Their loyalty to the regiment and bravery in conflict over almost seven decades was outstanding, as clearly evidenced in the Honours and Awards appendix to the back of this book.

I salute them and their memory.

Brigadier F.G.D. Heppenstall MLM
Lymington
Hampshire
UK
March 2015

Glossary

A Cpl	Acting Corporal
BCR	Bronze Cross of Rhodesia
Bn	Battalion
Brig	Brigadier
BSAP	British South Africa Police
Capt	Captain
CO	Commanding Officer
Col	Colonel
C Sgt	Colour Sergeant
COMOPS	Combined Operations
Coy	Company
Cpl	Corporal
CSM	Company Sergeant-Major
CT	communist terrorist
CWGC	Commonwealth War Graves Commission
DCD	Defence Cross for Distinguished Service
DMM	Defence Force Medal for Meritorious Service
DOAS	Died on Active Service
FAF	forward airfield
FN FAL	*Fabrique Nationale Fusil Automatique Léger*, standard Rhodesian infantry weapon
FN MAG	*Mitrailleuse d'Appui Général*, standard Rhodesian light machine gun
Ft	fort
GEA	German East Africa
Indep	Independent
Intaf	Internal Affairs
ISO	Imperial Service Order
JOC	Joint Operations Centre/Command
K-car	helicopter gunship
KIA	Killed in Action
KOAS	Killed on Active Service
L Cpl	Lance-Corporal
Lt	Lieutenant
Lt-Col	Lieutenant-Colonel
Maj	Major
MBE	Member of the Most Excellent Order of the British Empire
MFC	Military Forces Commendation
MIA	Missing in Action
MID	Military Intelligence Department
MLM	Member of the Legion of Merit
MSM	Meritorious Service Medal
MTO	Motor Transport Officer
NAZ	National Archives of Zimbabwe
N Cst	Native Constable
NRR	Northern Rhodesia Regiment
N Sgt	Native Sergeant
OC	Officer Commanding
OBE	Officer of the Most Excellent Order of the British Empire
OLM	Officer of the Legion of Merit
Op	operation
Para	paratrooper
PEA	Portuguese East Africa
Pl	platoon
Pte	Private
Rct	recruit
Regt	Regiment
Rfn	Rifleman
RhAEC	Rhodesian Army Education Corps
RhAMC	Rhodesian Army Medical Corps
RhAPC	Rhodesian Army Pay Corps
RhCCh	Rhodesian Corps of Chaplains
RL	Heavy troop carrier
RLI	Rhodesian Light Infantry
RQMS	Regimental Quarter Master Sergeant
RR	Rhodesia Regiment
RSM	Regimental Sergeant-Major
SAS	Special Air Service (C Squadron)
SCR	Silver Cross of Rhodesia
Sgt	Sergeant
Sp	Support
T 2Lt	Temporary Second Lieutenant
T Cpl	Temporary Corporal
TTL	Tribal Trust Land
UNIP	United National Independence Party, Northern Rhodesia (now Zambia)
VC	Victoria Cross
WOI	Warrant Officer Class 1
WOII	Warrant Officer Class 2
ZANLA	Zimbabwe African National Liberation Army
ZANU	Zimbabwe African National Union
ZAPU	Zimbabwe African People's Union
ZIPRA	Zimbabwe People's Revolutionary Army

Introduction

Over the years since 1980 when Rhodesia became Zimbabwe, much has been written about the various regiments that served the country of Rhodesia; from the early pioneers in the 1890s, right through to the day that these fine units marched off their respective parade grounds for the last time into the august annals of history. Much of this service for the older regiments, such as the Rhodesia Regiment, the British South Africa Police, the Rhodesia Native Regiment and the Rhodesian African Rifles, was as a contribution to the British Empire's war efforts during the South African War, both World Wars, and other regional conflicts of the 1950s and 1960s.

This Book of Remembrance, however, has been specifically compiled as a lasting tribute to the men of the Rhodesia Native Regiment (RNR) and its successor, the Rhodesian African Rifles (RAR) who, during the proud and honourable life of these units, made the ultimate sacrifice. It is not a definitive history of these regiments, as this has been admirably done in books such as *Masodja* and *Ragtime Soldiers,* to mention just a couple.

Accordingly, the book briefly looks at the history of each of the regiments and their battalions, with pictorial depictions of uniforms, badges, theatres of operation and colours. Chapters are also dedicated to those who received honours and awards for bravery and dedication to duty, with citations where it has been possible to source.

The main content is the various rolls of honour, covering all the major conflicts and areas of operation in which the two units saw active service. Differing from the standard impersonal lists of names and numbers, where possible, the rolls carry more information about causes of death and places of final burial, important aspects of personalising individual entries. The book will therefore itself be a memorial record for generations to come.

The Rhodesian African Rifles Regimental Association (UK) has made the decision to erect a memorial to the RNR and RAR at the National Memorial Arboretum near Alrewas in England, already the home to a fine memorial to the British South Africa Police. In April 2012, a tree-planting ceremony was held on the grounds of the 150-acre NMA to commemorate these two regiments. A plaque next to the tree honours those of the RNR and RAR who served Crown and country.

In May 2012, Brigadier David Heppenstall, former commanding officer of 1st Battalion RAR, approached me to see if I would author a book of remembrance. The book would not only be used as an important fund-raiser for the NMA memorial, but will be deposited in the NMA Chapel as part of our sacred duty to those of the RNR and RAR who paid the ultimate sacrifice for their country and for mankind. Having recently published with Adrian Haggett, the *Combined Rhodesian Forces Roll of Honour 1966–1981*, many of the important elements were in place, so I accepted the honour and privilege to help preserve the memory of those brave men of the Rhodesia Native Regiment and Rhodesian African Rifles.

Ndichakutengera sweet banana.

Gerry van Tonder
Derby, England
April 2015

Chapter 1

A Brief History of the RNR

Introduction

During the Great War, a private chartered company, the British South Africa Company, administered Southern Rhodesia (now Zimbabwe). As the objective of this company was to return dividends to its shareholders, the entry into the war of Southern Rhodesia units was inevitably delayed by financial wrangling between the company and the British government. When it had been established that the military recruitment of white soldiers from Southern Rhodesia had exhausted the available supply, attention was turned to the recruitment of Africans. This was not an easy political step to take, as although Northern Rhodesia to the north (now Zambia) and Nyasaland to the northeast (now Malawi) recruited Africans for their military units, the white settlers in Southern Rhodesia had always resisted 'arming the natives', other than in small auxiliary units.

However, more infantrymen were needed for operations on the Nyasaland and Northern Rhodesia borders with German East Africa. In November 1915, the Rhodesian forces, commanded by Colonel A.H.M. Edwards, proposed that an African battalion be raised in Southern Rhodesia. The War Office in Britain asked the British South Africa Company to facilitate, and after several months of haggling and prevarication, the company finally agreed to provide the men, subject to reimbursement of all costs involved.

It was initially planned for the soldiers to be recruited from the amaNdebele tribe, so the new unit was titled the Matabele Regiment. Officers and senior ranks were recruited from the Southern Rhodesia Native Affairs Department and the British South Africa Police.

Lieutenant-Colonel Alfred James Tomlinson, British South Africa Police, was appointed the commanding officer. African rates of pay were twenty-five shillings per month for privates and thirty shillings for sergeants. A gratuity of ten pounds was fixed for the next of kin of any soldier who died during service. An award of ten pounds and an exemption from hut tax was decreed for any recipient of the Distinguished Conduct Medal (DCM). Those men partially disabled due to war service would also qualify for a ten-pound compensation payment, while those permanently disabled would receive a pension of three pounds per month. Europeans were placed on the British South Africa Police pay scale, where a sergeant was paid 180 shillings a month and a lieutenant 250 pounds a year.

On 1 May 1916, 132 Africans and twenty-seven Europeans moved into a tented camp at Letomba, and training commenced. The Africans were issued with khaki shorts, jumper and cap, but no footwear. The first rifles issued were single-shot Martini Henrys dating back to the Zulu War. The first sets of equipment were leather ones. It was soon realized that the recruitment of 500 amaNdebele was not going to be achieved, as labour was scarce due to the Southern Rhodesian economy having been boosted by the war. European employers producing crops, goods and services for the war effort wanted to keep hold of their African labour. Also, many Africans preferred to work on their tribal holdings of land rather than work for wages. Men came forward from the Mashona ethnic group, and many others were recruited from mine compounds, with the agreement of the mining companies. Most of these former miners were migrant workers from Nyasaland, Northern Rhodesia and Portuguese East Africa (now Mozambique). Nearly all the recruits were illiterate, as the educated Southern Rhodesian Africans were not attracted towards military service. The variety of dialects being spoken resulted in the two companies that were formed being manned by men from the same tribal groupings where possible. The unit was retitled The Rhodesia Native Regiment.

Into German East Africa

By July 1916, 426 Africans had been recruited, and were in various stages of training. Suitable junior non-commissioned officers were found amongst men who had previously served in the British South Africa Native Police, the Northern Rhodesia Police and the King's African Rifles. General Edward Northey, the commander of the Nyasaland-Rhodesia Field Force, had an urgent requirement for troops, so the battalion was dispatched to Nyasaland using the rail, coastal shipping and river steamer route through Beira and Chinde in Portuguese East Africa. Between 26 July and 17 August, training was continued at Zomba, the centre of the 1st King's African Rifles.

On 18th August, the unit marched to Lake Nyasa, and from there travelled by the steamer *Guendolen* to the head of the lake. It then marched to New Langenburg in occupied German East Africa to continue training.

Here a modified range course was carried out, using the Martini Henry rifles. New webbing and equipment was issued and specialist sub-units formed. Six machine guns were issued and teams for them trained. Signallers learned to use flags and Begbie signal lamps. Superstition initially handicapped the use of heliograph mirrors and sunlight, but this problem was overcome. A demonstration was given on the use of the rifle grenade, but there were insufficient grenades for individual practice. Patrols, company attacks and the digging of defensive positions were rehearsed, and numerous route marches executed. An important aspect of the training was the instruction on military tactics and leadership given to European junior officers and sergeants, as many of them had been immediately promoted from the previous rank of trooper in the British South African Police.

While in Nyasaland, malaria had begun to affect and debilitate the unit. On 1 September 1916, the strength return of the Rhodesia Native Regiment listed seventeen European officers, forty-three European senior ranks and 442 African troops.

Operations commence

General Northey had hoped that Portugal, now an ally, would send troops north from Portuguese East Africa to occupy the south-eastern area of German East Africa. However, the Portuguese commander, Major-General Ferreira Gil, did not receive all the elements of his expeditionary force from Lisbon until early September, so he was unable – and unwilling – to comply with the British request. Gil's preference had been to advance up the German coastline so that his naval assets could be used, but he was ill equipped to advance inland through difficult terrain. However, the British had occupied the important ports and harbours in southern German East Africa, so for the moment the Portuguese remained on the north bank of the Rovuma River, near the coast.

Northey then decided to use his only reserve, the partially trained Rhodesia Native Regiment, to seize Songea, east of Lake Nyasa. On 14 September, Tomlinson was ordered to move his headquarters and one of his two companies from New Langenburg. He again travelled by the steamer *Guendolen* to Wiedhaven, from where he would march to Songea "in order to deny it to the enemy". As only one of the two companies, No. 1 Company under Major F.H. Addison, had so far exchanged its old rifles for Short Magazine Lee Enfields (SMLE), that company was selected to move. Because machine-gun porters had not yet arrived at the battalion, none of the guns was taken. No. 2 Company remained at New Langenburg under the command of Major Clive Lancaster Carbutt, who continued the training programme. When eighty machine-gun porters arrived, Carbutt organized their training so that the porters could be integrated into the gun teams.

The advance on Songea

Tomlinson was urgently dispatched into relatively unknown territory without machine guns and without the support of any other unit. However, the Allied theatre commander, the South African General Jan Christian Smuts, wanted to prevent south-eastern German East Africa becoming a sanctuary where the withdrawing enemy *Schütztruppe* under Colonel Paul von Lettow-Vorbeck could rest and regroup. The Germans occupied Songea, a rich farming area, but the strength of the garrison was not known.

No. 1 Company was accompanied by 176 supply porters known as 'Tenga-Tenga'. Thirty-five Africans, who resided in the Songea area, and who were now working as scouts for Tomlinson's intelligence section, also joined No. 1 Company. Captain James Joseph McCarthy MC, from the Northern Rhodesia Police, commanded the sub-unit. Northey's headquarters allocated an officer to command the supply base at Wiedhaven, another to control the porters, and a third Swahili-speaking officer, Captain Charles Grey, to join the battalion as an intelligence officer.

On 16 September, Captain F.J. Wane made a tactical landing at Wiedhaven, with half of No. 1 Company and the scouts. When the area was reported clear of the enemy, the remainder of the troops, porters and supplies were landed. A German patrol of ten Askari, commanded by Sergeant Lindemann, observed the landing but did not engage the Rhodesians. McCarthy set out with his scouts and twenty soldiers to reconnoitre the track to Songea. Later in the afternoon, Tomlinson, followed with a main body of twenty-nine Europeans, 165 African soldiers and a column of porters. He was planning to march through the night.

However, the soldiers, and especially the scouts, were only partly trained, so inexperience and apprehension prevailed. Around midnight, four highly agitated scouts ran back into the main body, shouting that they had fired on a small German-led patrol. This unsettled the soldiers so much, that Tomlinson soon halted and waited for dawn in order to avoid walking into an enemy ambush. He resumed the march at 0530 hours. Later that morning he caught up with McCarthy, who had slowed down because of nervousness amongst his party. In fact, the Germans were withdrawing ahead of McCarthy's scouts, and they did not want a contact as they had demolition tasks to perform on the track ahead.

That afternoon, Tomlinson ordered the signal section to establish a heliograph post under Sergeant Clegg on the nearby Namusweya Mountain, which had line of sight to Wiedhaven. As the porters were slowing down due to the hilly terrain, the column was split. Major Addison commanded the main body, while Tomlinson moved ahead, marching through the night with an advance party of three Europeans, thirty soldiers and McCarthy's scouts. On 18 September, the advance party came across bridges that had been burned by the withdrawing enemy. Improvised crossings were made using poles for support. The men gained some rest when a cow was acquired from local herdsmen and slaughtered for a meal. That afternoon, a few shots were fired at the scouts, but Tomlinson again pressed on by marching through the night.

Another hot day was spent marching and crossing the Rovuma River, where a strategic bridge had also been burned. The column had another opportunity to rest when maize was bought from farmers and a hot meal cooked. Hearing that there were Germans at the nearby Mangua Mission, Tomlinson advanced to the mission, where he found nine European missionaries, two male and seven nuns. He also discovered a large quantity of rations packed into loads and ready for removal. The rations were very welcome and the advance party stayed the night at the mission. McCarthy's scouts came in with news that the German troops at Songea were marching away.

The following morning, 20 September, Tomlinson entered Songea. Immediately prior to this, the scouts had established that the garrison of four Germans and thirty Askari had moved off towards Likuyu, over 160 kilometres to the northeast. The Rhodesia Native Regiment soldiers occupied the small Songea fortified post and brought in the missionaries with their livestock from Mangua. The next morning Addison and his main body arrived. No. 1 Company and the scouts and porters were exhausted having speed-marched and ascended over 500 metres to arrive at Songea.

The advance party had averaged over fifty kilometres per day. Tomlinson improved the Songea defences and commenced an intensive local patrol programme that went out as far as Kitanda and the Mbarangandu River. Local farmers came in to exchange cattle and produce for measures of cloth that had been brought for such trading purposes. The signals section established additional heliograph posts and established contact with its isolated detachment on Namusweya Mountain, putting Tomlinson in touch with Wiedhaven and through that base to Northey's headquarters.

Local chiefs came in to accept British authority, requesting that the destroyed bridges be rebuilt, which was also one of Tomlinson's priorities. The Germans had no field companies in the area, so they had been caught off-balance by the landing at Wiedhaven and the advance on Songea. But they had already started to plan retaliation.

No. 2 Company goes into action

Meanwhile back at New Langenburg, Carbutt continued training No. 2 Company and the machine-gun teams. But as German troops from Tabora descended onto the British lines of communication, Northey had to deploy No. 2 Company onto guarding supply dumps. On 11 October 1916, Carbutt was ordered to march with his men and four machine guns to garrison New Utengule. When a detachment of 29 Field Company came into the area, two of Carbutt's platoons pursued it to Buhora, which they occupied. Another platoon was employed to escort on motor convoys moving between Buhora and Malangali.

On 23 October, one of the Buhora platoons, commanded by Lieutenant William Benzies and entrenched at the village of Maborgoro, was attacked by German troops led by Major Max Wintgens. Benzies had with him three European sergeants and eighteen soldiers, and had been ordered to dig in and await further orders. A circular firing position was dug, using farmers' hoes, the only digging implements issued. The machine gun was placed in the centre. A German field company approached through the bush to the rear of the position and attacked at 0800 hours. The defenders fought for six hours until the machine gun was hit in the breech, jamming it. The platoon was then surrounded by enemy Askari, appearing out of the smoke of a bush fire that had started.

Three privates, Sikoti, Mangwana and Bidu were killed and Corporal Zakeyo, the machine-gunner, was wounded, along with Sergeants Childs and Merrington. Benzies and the remainder of his platoon were taken prisoner. The Germans had lost several men killed and their Askari wanted revenge. If Benzies had not surrendered, then it is likely that there would have been very few, if any, Rhodesian survivors.

In early November, enemy units under Major-General Kurt Wahle threatened a British supply base at Malangali. The base was not on the rocky ground that had been defended when the British first seized Malangali, but in a hollow overlooked by higher ground. The only infantry troops at Malangali were fifty men of the 2nd South African Rifles under Captain Tom Marriott. Carbutt was ordered to send from Buhora men and machine guns under Lieutenant William Baker to strengthen the garrison, bringing Marriott's strength up to 100 men and two machine guns. Malangali had to be held because it was the base that the South African troops in Iringa depended upon.

The defence of Malangali

On 7 November, Wahle's scouts were in position, observing the British at Malangali. The next day an attack, using artillery and machine guns, began. The British telegraph line was cut and fire was directed into the perimeter from all sides. On the 9th, more German troops, under Captain Erich von Langenn-Steinkeller, joined Wahle. Bayonet assaults were launched. A German shell, fired from one of the British naval guns captured at Ngominyi, set the supply dump alight, burning rations and illuminating the British position during the hours of darkness.

The Germans mounted three assaults, but all were repulsed with loss to the attackers. The machine guns of the Rhodesia Native Regiment were handled well, their fire preventing the German troops from breaking into the perimeter. Northey was now arranging infantry support, utilizing the roads that South African engineers and African labour had just completed from New Langenburg towards Iringa and Lupembe. Components for fifty light Hupmobile and Ford lorries had arrived in Nyasaland where they had been assembled. These vehicles were driven to Lupembe, where they joined Murray's Rhodesian column late on 8 September.

At dawn the next morning, a column of 100 men of the British South Africa Police, thirty of the Northern Rhodesia Police, armed with four machine guns, drove to within three kilometres of Malangali, where they debussed and bivouacked for the night. Murray sent the vehicles back to Buhora for supplies.

Meanwhile, Captain Charles Henry Fair, Northern Rhodesia Police, had been marching for two days from the east with his company towards Malangali. Fair arrived in the area on the 8th, but he was unaware of Murray's imminent arrival by motor transport. Both Fair and Murray assessed that Wahle's force was too strong for a successful British attack.

A turning point in the battle came when Wahle learned that one of his companies to the east had made contact with German troops under Major Georg Kraut. The Germans had withdrawn from the British forces in the Kidatu region, south of Morogoro on the central railway. Wahle then prepared to march with the bulk of his troops to join Kraut, leaving the 26th Field Company to contain Malangali, and hopefully starve it into surrender.

After reconnoitring separately for twenty-four hours, Fair and Murray encountered each other and joined forces. On 12 September, the fifth day of the Malangali siege, a successful attack was made on the 26th Field Company, which by now was withdrawing to be Wahle's rearguard, only losing four men wounded. Murray and Fair killed two Germans and nine Askari, and captured seven Germans, ten Askari, seventy-two porters, one machine gun, thirty-nine cattle and fifteen donkeys and mules. The abortive siege of Malangali had ended with the Germans sustaining thirty-eight casualties.

A lone British aeroplane had appeared in the sky on 12 November, and with rudimentary bombs, it engaged the enemy. This alarmed the German Askari but cheered up the British troops at Malangali. Within the perimeter, the Rhodesia Native Regiment had lost Private Mbujane, killed when he was shot in the head by a sniper; two others were wounded. One other defender had been killed and two wounded. These light losses can be attributed to well-constructed trenches and fire positions and to sound management of the defensive battle.

Captain Tom Marriott, South African Rifles, was later awarded a Military Cross for conspicuous gallantry during an enemy attack on the garrison, which he was commanding. The attacking force, with artillery, was far superior in number, but by Captain Marriott's energy in organizing the defence and by his fine example of coolness and courage, he held the post. They repulsed three enemy assaults at close quarters, inflicting severe losses on the enemy. Marriott, who had been wounded and evacuated as a casualty from the first battle of Malangali on 24–25 July, was only there for the siege as he was passing through from hospital to rejoin his unit. As the German threat became apparent, Northey sent a telegram on 2 November ordering Marriott to command the post at Malangali. Of the Rhodesia Native Regiment defenders, Marriott praised Lieutenant William Baker and Sergeant-Major William John Carr, who was later commissioned. Both Baker and Carr were later awarded the French *Croix de Guerre*.

Another man who had pleased Marriott during the defence was Sergeant Frederick Charles Booth, who was soon to become the most famous member of the Rhodesia Native Regiment. All three men were to be mentioned in despatches. Whilst Marriott did not mention the Rhodesian soldiers, Baker in his report did, stating, "The native troops reserved their fire and took good aim, whilst the fire control generally exercised was of a high order. The maxims were most efficiently worked and were the main factors in each instance in breaking up the attack".

Activities around Songea

Further south in Songea, Tomlinson and No. 1 Company, although still without machine guns, were actively patrolling with McCarthy's scouts. This intense patrolling paid dividends. Local villagers who had endured hardship in the past when the Germans conscripted porters and requisitioned crops welcomed the British presence.

A steady supply of sound information started coming in from the local people. Europeans commanded most patrols, but Tomlinson started tasking two literate African non-commissioned officers as commanders: Corporals Lita and Tanganyika. Both men performed well at penetrating enemy-dominated areas and at sending written reports back to Tomlinson. Other useful patrol commanders were Corporals Salima, Juma and Paisha. Lita, Tanganyika and Salima each captured prisoners who provided good information on German movements and intentions.

By the end of October, it was evident that German strengths in the area were increasing. British patrols were being pushed back down the roads from Likuyu and Kitanda, during which four Rhodesian soldiers were killed. Tomlinson was ordered by Northey to hold Songea at all costs. The Rhodesia Native Regiment improved the defences of Songea fort by demolishing houses that blocked fields of fire and by digging more surrounding trenches. Barbed wire left behind by the Germans was erected outside the perimeter.

Regimental Sergeant-Major Usher was tasked with getting more stocks of reserve ammunition up the track from Wiedhaven. As villagers reported that German patrols were searching for the British 'lights', the four isolated heliograph relay stations linking Songea to Wiedhaven were permitted to withdraw if enemy troops approached them. A party of 200 porters brought in stocks of grain from the nearby Peramiho Mission, and within the Songea perimeter, every available container was filled with water.

Reinforcements from South Africa

Smuts, farther north in German East Africa, appreciated the weakness in the Songea area so he dispatched an infantry battalion to reinforce Northey's command. The unit chosen was the 5th South African Infantry under Lieutenant-Colonel John Joseph Byron CMG. Byron moved from Morogoro to Dar es Salaam where he embarked his men on 16 October. However, disease and casualties had reduced the battalion to only 150 men. The troopship was sent to Durban to take on board 600 recruits before it sailed north again to disembark the strengthened battalion at Chinde.

Unfortunately, many of these white South African recruits were barely trained. Many had been enlisted without stringent medical examinations. Both these factors were to present Byron with problems in the field.

The German attack on Songea

Von Lettow-Vorbeck had ordered two groups of troops to cooperate in retaking Songea. At Kitanda, Captain Walter von Falkenstein was to advance with the 12th Field Company and the former Songea garrison. At Likuyu, Major Gideon von Grawert was to advance with the 7th Schützen Company of German reservists and the Penzel's detachment. Von Grawert was appointed to command the attack on Songea.

On 11 November, von Falkenstein's troops approached Songea, while one of his patrols successfully ambushed a British resupply column on the Wiedhaven track. The porters dropped the four-day supply of rations they were carrying and ran to Songea. Perhaps due to misinformation from local villagers, but von Falkenstein had come to believe that the British garrison was weak and ill trained. He was also an impatient man. He did not wait for von Grawert, but attacked at first light on 12 November with his 180 men and one machine gun.

The German attack came in from the southeast just as the Rhodesia Native Regiment 'stood to' in an alert position in their trenches. The German machine gun jammed after only firing a few bursts, and from then on both sides depended upon the weight and accuracy of their rifle fire. The advantage lay with the defenders as von Falkenstein had lost the element of surprise.

Whilst engaging the withdrawing enemy machine-gunners, Captain Wane was shot in the shoulder. A drummer in the regimental band, Private Rupea, was shot and killed while defending the eastern section of the perimeter. A number of villagers and porters added confusion to the battlefield by being shot as they ran to jump into the Rhodesian trenches. A party of German troops had been seen entering a hospital building that overlooked the trenches, so Sergeant Charles Craxton and four soldiers ran forward 350 metres to set the roof of the building on fire. The enemy party hastily evacuated the building. For this gallantry, Craxton was awarded the Military Medal.

Around noon, von Grawert arrived on the scene. With a machine gun firing effectively in support, his more than 200 men attacked from the north and east. However, the Germans could not neutralize the Rhodesian rifle fire or the rifle grenades that the defenders fired. The attackers failed to get through the barbed wire and into the British trenches. At dusk, with his ammunition stocks running low, von Grawert withdrew three kilometres to Unangwa Hill, which overlooked Songea. Von Falkenstein and seven Askari lay dead, and another officer and twelve Askari had been wounded. The Rhodesians had taken one more casualty, Private Chewa, who had sustained a head wound.

During the next four days, both sides patrolled against and sniped at each other. Von Grawert withdrew a farther ten kilometres to Nyambengo. He did not attempt to disrupt the Rhodesian heliograph link, allowing Tomlinson to receive news that a relief force of South African infantry was on its way. The signals sergeant responsible for maintaining the heliograph link, L.C. Symonds, was to later be mentioned in despatches and to receive the French *Medaille Militaire*.

On 18 November, violent thunderstorms delivered heavy rainfalls that flooded the trenches, as well as negating the heliographs. At 1130 hours, von Grawert used the opportune weather to again attack from the north, but his men were pushed back after only ten minutes of fighting. Patrolling then continued, in which Corporal Lita stood out. He later received an Imperial Distinguished Conduct Medal for conspicuous gallantry in action on several occasions. His example and influence with his men was incalculable.

Byron and 350 men of his 5th South African Infantry with two machine guns arrived at Songea on 24 November, and German activity in the area decreased. Byron took over command of the garrison.

Conclusion

Tomlinson could be proud of the performance of his men and their European officers and sergeants. All ranks had exercised good fire discipline, using only rifles and grenades, which had resulted in a controlled conservation of ammunition and a successful defence with minimal casualties. The Rhodesia Native Regiment, both at Songea and farther north at Malangali, had come to terms with the enemy and battlefield conditions. The unit's self-confidence and morale was high. However, tougher marches and battles loomed ahead. A few weeks after their capture at Maborgoro, William Benzies and his men either escaped or were allowed to leave captivity. They rejoined the British forces.

Towards the end of 1918, an exhausted regiment returned to Ntondwe, south of Zomba in Nyasaland, having been part of the force that had pursued the elusive von Lettow-Vorbeck through large tracts of German and Portuguese East Africa. The regiment had given an extremely good account of itself in this theatre of operation, earning its successor, the RAR, the right to carry the battle honours 'The Great War' and 'East Africa 1916-1918' on its regimental colours.

In December, the regiment returned to Salisbury where it was officially disbanded. It had lost 160 men killed in action or having died from disease such as the Spanish Influenza pandemic that swept the world in 1918.

A message was sent to King George V from the chiefs of Rhodesia with a loyal and moving declaration from the askaris of the RNR: "We wish to say that, when the King called upon us for help, we sent our young men, who fought and died beside the English, and we claim that our blood and that of the English are now one".

2RNR

In the meantime, on 16 September 1917, Major Addison of 1RNR left Rhodesia with a batch of newly trained 2RNR men, to bring 1RNR up to strength in the East Africa theatre. Numbering seventy-five Europeans and 585 askaris, commanded by Major Jackson, the men were trooped by train to Beira in Portuguese East Africa. From there, they left for Chinde on the steamer *Ipu*, and on 21 September, they boarded the riverboats *Empress* and *Chipandi* at the mouth of the Zambezi River, bound for the railhead at Chindio, from where they would be taken by train to Limbe in Nyasaland (now Malawi).

The battalion left Limbe on 29 September for Ntondwe, there to await further orders. Here the troops' normal routine and training regimes were adapted to acclimatize the men to the unaccustomed high temperatures.

The battalion left Ntondwe on 10 October, arriving at Mbewa on the north-eastern shore of Lake Nyasa six days later, having left a number of sick at Zomba. At Mbewa, the troops spent the next four weeks constructing a camp.

At this time, Major du Frere arrived at the 2RNR camp, with orders to improve the battalion's machine-gun section. He dispatched Second Lieutenant Church, together with Sergeants Jule and Musgrave, to Blantyre for a week's instruction on Lewis machine guns.

In mid-November, the battalion recommenced training, including company and platoon drill, which was followed with daily fieldwork. Drill and musketry took place in the latter half of the month, as the battalion awaited their deployment orders.

On 30 November, Major F.J. Wane arrived to assume duty as Battalion 2IC. Wane would later go on to perform the task of forming 1RAR. Orders were eventually received for the battalion to move to Mhamba Bay, but the possibility of a German patrol passing through Nyasaland prevented the deployment. However, patrols sent out to check on this intelligence returned on 12 December, having seen nothing of the enemy. Wane commenced field training for his troops, based on his own experiences in the region. The askaris were all issued with 150 rounds of ammunition, which was the first time they had to carry such large quantities.

On 20 December, the battalion was readied to sail in two batches on 30 December and 3 January. On 24 December, a four-man patrol was sent north to look for any signs of the enemy. In spite of a heavy downpour, Christmas Day was spent on sporting activities, and on 30 December, the first batch of troops sailed for Mhamba Bay, arriving there the following morning. On 28 January 1918, 2RNR was amalgamated with its sister battalion, 1RNR, the combined force being titled the 2nd Rhodesia Native Regiment.

The new regiment, armed with new Lewis machine guns, now made for Portuguese East Africa (now Mozambique), to join in chasing down the elusive German commander Lieutenant-Colonel Paul von Lettow-Vorbeck and his *Schütztruppen*. They were now in an area bordered to the north and south by the Rovuma and Luria rivers respectively, and to the west by Lake Nyasa, with the Indian Ocean to the east.

With many of the officers and askari now suffering from malaria and dysentery, during the first half of February the regiment marched up the eastern shores of Lake Nyasa to Mtengula. The RNR now fell under Colonel Clayton, the column commander of the 2nd Cape Corps, while Major Wane was appointed column staff officer. The troops were tasked to relocate the hospital at Mhamba to Mtengula.

The regiment then moved to Mwembe, 180 miles to the east, and from there to Mtarika on the Lujenda River, some 120 miles away. Here they found the Cape Corps badly decimated by illness, requiring the regiment to relieve the Cape Corps at Chisona.

Responding to intelligence of a German presence on the Niare River, an RNR company under Captain Bugler was immediately sent out, accompanied by a force of Cape Corps commanded by Major Fraser. This combined force linked up with a company of King's African Rifles, under Colonel Griffith, who took overall command. On 22 May, they took a German supply column, capturing two German officers, two German askaris, and thirty-four Portuguese askaris and 252 porters. Realizing that they had arrived in between von Lettow-Vorbeck's main column and his rearguard, the troops quickly started to dig in and consolidate their position.

Not much later, the entrenched troops found themselves under attack from the main German column on the one side, and the rearguard on the other. Fighting continued until last light, during which time many casualties were sustained. The RNR stood firm throughout. Sergeant Lungwe in particular was conspicuous, moving about under heavy fire, encouraging his men and directing their fire. As darkness fell, the Germans broke off their attack, and continued marching south.

At Mtarika, the much-depleted RNR undertook active patrolling and the escorting of food convoys to Mwanza. On 30, the regiment was given orders to proceed to Mahua, as the Germans were operating many miles to the south. By 23 July, they reached Mocubi, where an accidental mortar bomb explosion resulted in the tragic deaths of Lieutenants Hopkins and Durrant, five troops of the Cape Corps, and an askari.

Continuing their pursuit of von Lettow-Vorbeck, the RNR crossed the Luo and Licingu rivers, and on 1 August, they halted at Inagu, where the askaris were issued with much overdue replacement uniforms. The Ligonha River crossing occurred on 8 August, where General Edwards congratulated them on their speedy march. The RNR took up a position on the Ligonha's west bank, also placing two platoons in an old fort half a mile away.

The exhausting cat-and-mouse chase continued, and when the RNR reached Alto Ligonha in mid-August, the regiment was brigaded with the KAR, commanded by Colonel Shorthorn.

At 0200 hours on 25 August , with the RNR as advance guard, the column marched off, and crossing the Licingu River, they found the telegraph lines had been cut by the Germans. The RNR's forward patrols had running skirmishes with the enemy, during which two sergeants were killed.

On 27 August, the force reached the abandoned German post at Nhamarrhoi Boma, where they found thirty wounded men hiding, and captured a German officer. Fleeting skirmishes and isolated contacts in the area of the Lurio and Luelo rivers, marked the RNR's final involvement in the war.

The map in Appendix V gives a clearer picture of the mammoth distances – way in excess of 2,000 miles – the RNR marched in pursuit of the Germans. Von Lettow-Vorbeck, however, eluded his enemy to the end, finally surrendering, after the Armistice in Europe, at Abercorn in Northern Rhodesia (now Zambia) on 25 November 1918.

The regiment retired to camp at Ntondwe, near Zomba, where the devastating Spanish flu pandemic of 1918, took the lives of scores of RNR troops.

In December 1918, the RNR arrived back in Salisbury, where the regiment was disbanded. However, the brave conduct of the regiment would not be forgotten. In 1952, the successor to the Rhodesia Native Regiment, the Rhodesian African Rifles, was granted permission to emblazon their colours with the RNR honours: 'The Great War' and 'East Africa 1916–18'.

Original Officers 1RNR 1916. Back row from left: Capt A. J. Poole, Lt F. W. C.Morgans, Lt A. H. Rutherford (KIA), Lt W. R. Benzies (wounded), Lt J. H. Williams (KIA), Lt E. F. Bridges (died of wounds), Capt W. J. Baker (KIA), Lt F. P. L. Piggin (KIA). Front row: Capt F. C. Burke (wounded), Capt V. A. New, Maj C. L. Carbutt, Lt-Col A. J. Tomlinson, Maj E. H. Addison, Lt H. J. Simpson (KIA) and Capt F. J. Wane (wounded)

1RNR marching through Salisbury shortly after the unit was formed 1916.

1RNR at the port of Chinde at the mouth of the Zambezi en route to Nyasaland 1916.

Lt F.W.C. Morgans. Most ops photos in German East Africa were taken by him.

1RNR at Fort Johnston en route to German East Africa via Lake Nyasa 1916.

Elements of 1RNR going ashore at Mwaya at the north end of Lake Nyasa 1916.

Colonel the Honourable J.H.J.Byron (later General) and his staff watch the effect of gunfire by a mountain battery on German positions near Songea.

1RNR and their *tenga-tenga* (bearers) prepare to leave Songea (early 1917).

Captured German artillery piece at Songea 1916.

Captured German artillery at Songea 1916.

On operations, a ten-minute halt in German East Africa 1917.

1RNR detachment ready to march, German East Africa 1917. Front: Maj. C. L. Carbutt, Capt. W. J. Baker (KIA) and Lt. H. J. Simpson (KIA). Standing behind them from left are sergeants Baker and Barker.

The Machine Gun Platoon BNCO's 1RNR German East Africa 1917.

1RNR Medals Parade German East Africa 1917.

Column of porters (*tenga-tenga*) German East Africa 1917.

1RNR Mobile Column Songea 1917.

A baggage train (*tenga-tenga*) in German East Africa 1917.

Escorting German Prisoners German East Africa 1917.

2RNR and their *tenga-tenga* on the march towards Mwembe in Portuguese East Africa early in 1918.

The War Memorial Cross on the kopje between Umtali and Mozambique border to honour Rhodesian and Portuguese African soldiers who lost their lives during the Great War.

RAR training for war. Borrowdale Camp 1942. Grenade training.

RAR training for war. Borrowdale Camp 1942. Vickers machine-gun training.

The Governor of Southern Rhodesia inspects the RAR.

RAR training for war. Borrowdale Camp 1942. Weapon stripping blindfolded.

RAR training for war. Borrowdale Camp 1942. Training on 3-inch mortar.

RAR training for war. Borrowdale Camp 1942. Drill on the square.

RAR training for war. Borrowdale Camp 1942. Aiming practice.

Chemical warfare training. Borrowdale Camp 1942.

RAR training for war. Borrowdale Camp 1942. 3-inch mortar and Boyes anti-tank rifle.

Above and top right: Assault course.

Passing-out parade. The Governor Sir Herbert Stanley KCMG takes the salute. Borrowdale Camp 1942.

Chapter 2

A Brief History of the RAR and Independent Companies

1st and 2nd Battalions

Before looking at the history of the RAR, which was first formed in June 1940 by Major Wane, one must appreciate the close links that this unit had with the Rhodesian Native Regiment. Formed in mid-1916, the RNR, during the WWI, fought with distinction against the elusive and skilful General Paul von Lettow-Vorbeck in German East Africa. Although this unit had long since been disbanded, it had provided an Askari unit in the British South African Police, and it was from this source that the first African NCOs were obtained to form the RAR in 1940.

Initially, it had been intended to name the unit the Rhodesian Native Regiment, but this proposal was eventually rejected. First of all, the name 'native' was unpopular amongst the majority of Africans, and secondly, it was felt that the initials 'RNR' had a nautical flavour inappropriate to land-locked Rhodesia.

Regulations were published in Government Gazette No. 374, dated 19 July 1940, for the establishment of one or more battalions of a native regiment to be styled the Rhodesian African Rifles. The regiment became part of Southern Rhodesia's contribution to the war effort. There was no shortage of willing volunteers. Nearly all the recruits came from Southern Rhodesia. They were predominately from two main tribal groups, the Mzezuru and the amaNdebele. It is of interest to note that one of the officers involved with the raising and training of the battalion was from the South Wales Borderers, with whom the regiment was to affiliate seventeen years later.

The first depot for the RAR was built by the soldiers themselves at Borrowdale, just outside Salisbury (now Harare). The officers and European other ranks were drawn mainly from the British South Africa Police and Native Department (later Ministry of Internal Affairs), and as such were well qualified to serve with African troops. The commanding officer was Lieutenant-Colonel F.J. Wane ISO, who had been second-in-command of the Rhodesian Native Regiment during the First World War. All the normal aspects of training were covered, and in addition, soldiers specialized in driving, signalling, first aid, handling support weapons, and the construction of field defences.

In 1942, the 1st Battalion carried out extensive exercises in the Eastern Districts, which culminated in a march from Umtali to Salisbury. The last stretch of forty-plus miles, from a farm near Marandellas to Salisbury was covered in eleven hours forty-seven minutes, which at the time was understood to be a British and Commonwealth army record.

During 1942, detachments of the 1st Battalion were employed in escorting Italian internees from Durban to internment camps at Gatooma, Umvuma and Fort Victoria. During the train journeys through Natal, the soldiers used to buy bananas at halts, and as a result, the tune 'Sweet Banana' came into being. The bandmaster of the day, Mr Brims, put the tune to music. It was subsequently approved by the Royal College of Music in London, and became the RAR Regimental March.

The 1st Battalion left Rhodesia in November 1943 for final training at Moshi in Kenya. Here it joined 31 (East Africa) Brigade. Lieutenant-Colonel J.M. Macdonald had assumed command prior to leaving Rhodesia.

The formation of the 2nd Battalion started in October 1943, with this unit continuing its training in Southern Rhodesia during 1944.

Early in 1944, Lieutenant-Colonel G.H.K. Goode CBE, DSO, assumed command of the 1st Battalion. Shortly thereafter, the battalion left East Africa for Ceylon (now Sri Lanka), where it became part of 22 (East Africa) Independent Brigade. Intensive brigade and divisional training was carried out before the battalion moved to Burma in November of the same year.

During 1945, the 1st Battalion was employed on active operations in clearing the Mayu Range in the Arakan, Ramree Island, the Taungup area, Pegu Yomas and on to the Taungoo–Mawghi road. The actions from the Tanlwe Chaung and up the Taungup feature were the highlights of the battalion's fighting, which involved operating through some of the worst terrain in Burma, during the hottest and most trying time of the year. The Japanese, although withdrawing, were fighting a stubborn rear-guard action on ground of their own choosing, with the result that the battalion suffered a number of casualties. In spite of this, the battalion gained a reputation for determined and effective action.

The 1st Battalion maintained its cheerfulness and high morale at all times, in spite of shelling, mortaring and difficulty of terrain. Subsequently, the battle honours 'Taungup', 'Arakan Beaches' and 'Burma 1944-45' were awarded by the Queen. Tanlwe Chaung was subsequently celebrated annually as Regimental Day on 26 April. The 2nd Battalion continued training in Southern Rhodesia during 1945, after which it was also employed in escorting internees and prisoners of war to Zonderwater and Port Elizabeth in South Africa.

After the war, the 1st Battalion moved to Rangoon in March 1946, before returning to Southern Rhodesia via Colombo and East Africa. They arrived back in Salisbury in May, with demobilization beginning the same month. The 2nd Battalion also began its demobilization at the same time, although three of its companies were amalgamated with the Rhodesian Air Askari Corps and continued to serve until 31 October 1946. Their disbandment was completed by 30 November of that year.

Recruiting for the re-establishment of the RAR began again in December 1946. The regiment was re-formed primarily to provide attested labour for the Rhodesian Air Training Scheme at air stations at Khumalo, Heany and Thornhill.

The depot for recruiting and training continued at the wartime site on the Borrowdale Road, Salisbury . During 1949, A, B and C Companies became operational again. These sub-units provided demonstration troops at various TF camps of training.

In 1951, B Company was retitled Support Company, and its soldiers trained on the 3-inch mortar, the Vickers machine gun and the six-pound anti-tank gun.

Towards the end of 1951, Egypt abrogated the Canal Treaty of 1936, which resulted in terrorism and a lack of civilian labour in the Canal Zone. Some four-hundred officers and men were sent to Egypt in January 1952 in a general duties capacity. The draft did sterling work assisting the Royal Engineers on road construction, and later carried out guard duties on important installations. Trackers from the battalion assisted the military police in apprehending Arabs thieving from British supply depots. The draft returned to Rhodesia in November 1952.

In 1953, at an impressive parade held at the Borrowdale Camp in Salisbury, Her Majesty Queen Elizabeth the Queen Mother, presented the 1st Battalion with the Queen's Colour and Regimental Colour. The colours were the first to be given to the regiment, and it is understood that this was the first occasion that a battalion in Rhodesia had received colours at the hands of royalty.

Borrowdale Camp in Salisbury was on municipal land, so it was decided to move the 1st Battalion to Heany, outside Bulawayo, where it would be able to have a permanent home of its own, later to be known as Methuen Barracks. The move of battalion headquarters, C, D, and HQ Companies, took place in the middle of 1954. A and B companies, however, went to Northern Rhodesia to fill the void caused by the departure of 1NRR for active service in Malaya. A Company was stationed at Lusaka, whilst B Company went to Bwana Mkubwa. Both arrived back in Rhodesia in 1955 where they rejoined the rest of the battalion at Heany, now renamed Llewellin Barracks.

In 1954, the 1st Battalion was invigorated by the news that it was to proceed to Malaya in early 1956 to take part in operations against the communist terrorists, commonly referred to as CTs. This was part of the Federation's contribution to Commonwealth defence.

For several years, African battalions had been on operations in Malaya, relieving each other in turn. With a real operational aim in view, the tempo of training stepped up and the number of volunteers increased. The accent was on anti-terrorist operations, which included patrolling, anti-ambush drills, and a general toughening up.

The whole of 1955 was spent on vigorous exercises, forced marches, and endless firing on the ranges. At the beginning of 1956, the advance party flew to Malaya to prepare for the battalion's arrival, while the main body marched to the Matopos and carried out its final training exercise.

In early April, the Governor-General, Lord Llewellin, took the salute at the battalion's farewell parade and, on 9 April 1956, the 1st Battalion marched through the streets of Bulawayo on the first stage of its journey to Malaya.

After a period of 'training and acclimatization' at the Far East Training Centre, at Kota Tinggi in Johore, the battalion mounted its first operation on 4 June 1956. It came out of the jungle for the last time on 19 January 1958.

Throughout almost the whole period, the battalion operated in deep jungle in Johore, Negri-Sembilan and South Panang. Largely, the efforts of the companies denied the terrorists the use of their deep-jungle havens and cultivations, necessitating their movement towards the edge where food-denial operations and extensive patrolling and ambushing took their toll.

Due to the size and nature of their area of operations, information and intelligence was hard to come by. This resulted in fewer contacts with the terrorists than was achieved by units operating on the jungle fringe, and although only fourteen terrorists were eliminated, the battalion's kill-to-contact ratio was as good as any other unit at that time. Within three months of the battalion's departure, Hor Lung, the South Malay bureau chief, surrendered with two hundred of his followers. Among the main reasons given for their surrender was the food-denial campaign, combined with harassment in the deep jungle. Several members of the battalion were decorated for their services in Malaya.

1RAR served in the same brigade as that other very fine unit, the 1st Battalion, the South Wales Borderers, and as a result of the friendship and close cooperation between the two, Her Majesty the Queen consented to the affiliation in 1957. In 1969, a victim of the British defence reductions, the South Wales Borderers amalgamated with the Welsh Regiment to become the Royal Regiment of Wales. It is partly as a result of this affiliation that the 1RAR mascot was a goat.

In 1958, the battalion returned from Malaya. Upon arriving back in Salisbury, the men paraded in front of the governor-general. They later marched through the City of Bulawayo before returning to Methuen Camp near Llewellin Barracks.

In February 1959, the 1st Battalion flew to Nyasaland to serve in the Nyasaland Emergency, where they carried out internal security operations, mainly in the Southern Province. All disturbances were dealt with quickly and efficiently. In 1960, the battalion again returned to that country, covering the period that Dr Hastings Banda and other detainees in Nyasaland were released from prison.

Later in 1960, disturbances, terrorism and intimidation by political agitators in Southern Rhodesia, necessitated the deployment of the battalion to maintain law and order in the suburban African townships.

In 1961, disturbances in Northern Rhodesia, engineered by UNIP, resulted in the battalion being sent to that country on internal security operations. During this period, the Katangese secessionist war broke out in the Congo, and the battalion was deployed on the Congolese border to control refugees and prevent any of the fighting in the Congo spilling over into the Federation. Close and unbroken links existed between the Rhodesian African Rifles and the two battalions of the Rhodesian Native Regiment, which rendered such outstanding service in East Africa during World War I. This resulted in approval being given in 1962, by the Governor-General and commander-in-chief, on behalf of Her Majesty the Queen, for the Rhodesian African Rifles to succeed to the RNR battle honours. These were 'The Great War' and 'East Africa 1916-1918', awarded to the 1st Battalion the Rhodesian Native Regiment, and the battle honours 'The Great War' and 'East Africa 1917-1918' awarded to the 2nd Battalion the Rhodesian Native Regiment. Authority was also given for these battle honours to be emblazoned on the Colours of the Rhodesian African Rifles.

On 31 December 1963, the Federation of Rhodesia and Nyasaland was dissolved. The battalion then became part of the Rhodesian army, and its size increased by the addition of a fifth company, E Company. Army HQ had recommended that a second battalion be formed, but this had not been acceptable to the politicians.

Although the smuggling of arms and terrorist incursions into the country had started in the early 1960s, the tempo was stepped up following the Unilateral Declaration of Independence (UDI) on 11 November 1965. The RAR first became involved in border control duties in 1965, and in anti-terrorist operations in Rhodesia in 1966. Operation *Vermin* was to teach the battalion many lessons on the use of radios, uniforms and equipment, air support, patrolling, ambushes, tracking, and the use of vehicle patrols. At this time it was recommended that Land Rovers or F25O 4x4 vehicles should he used instead of the Bedford 3-ton RL lorries. But with increased landmining of the roads, it was found later in the war, that larger troop-carrying vehicles could sustain mine blasts if adequately mine-protected.

In August 1967, the 1st Battalion took part in what was at that time the largest internal anti-terrorist operation, Operation *Nickel*. This was the largest ever experienced in the country and was, in fact, the first fighting to have taken place in Matabeleland since the rebellion of 1896. The battalion was engaged in fighting well-trained and well-equipped terrorists belonging to both the South African National Congress (SAANC) and the Zimbabwe African Peoples Union (ZAPU).

The 1st Battalion bore the brunt of this successful operation. Of the eighty-plus terrorists who entered Rhodesia east of Victoria Falls, nearly sixty were eliminated. The remainder fled into Botswana where they received prison sentences for illegal entry and carriage of arms. Two officers and several other ranks were killed during the course of the fighting. Many lessons were learned during this operation, which proved to be of considerable benefit not only to the regiment, but also to all other units of the Rhodesian army in operations which were to follow.

From 1968 to 1971, the 1st Battalion was involved in many other operations along the length of the Zambian border as well as one or two attempted incursions from Botswana. Several of these resulted in the total elimination of terrorist gangs from both ZAPU and ZANU.

From December 1972, when a guerrilla attack on the Altena Farm homestead in Centenary heralded a major and concerted increase in terrorist activities inside the country, the 1st Battalion had been continuously committed to the longest and largest operation yet to have taken place in the northeast border area against ZANLA. The regiment played a vital part in the elimination of large numbers of terrorists, with companies operating as far apart as the Angwa River to Mtoko and from the Chiweshe TTL to Rusambo. Many members of the regiment were decorated for gallantry.

Because of pressure from Army HQ in the light of Operation *Hurricane*, the government agreed to the formation of a second battalion. Early in 1975, the training wing of the 1st Battalion was substantially increased to cater for the necessity to train many more men.

A Company 2RAR was established in October 1975, under the command of Major André Dennison.

In November 1975, an embryo battalion headquarters was set up in Fort Victoria under a new battalion commander, Lieutenant-Colonel Peter Hosking. In November 1975, A Company was deployed under the newly established JOC *Thrasher* in the Manicaland area, whilst the new 2RAR battalion headquarters was settling into a temporary home in the showgrounds at Fort Victoria. Little time was wasted in getting the new battalion under way.

Incursions into the nearby Lowveld area of the Victoria Province in January–February 1976, saw the need for establishing a sub-JOC at Chiredzi, which was provided by the new 2RAR battalion headquarters. Their first base was the airfield just outside the small village of Chiredzi itself. Later on, they moved to the much larger airfield nearby, Buffalo Range, where they were given more semi-permanent buildings in lieu of the tents used in their initial deployment. In the meantime, other 2RAR companies were being formed and rapidly deployed as they completed their training.

B Company, under Major John Pritchard, was the next company to arrive in Fort Victoria, followed by C Company under Major Nick Fawcett, D Company under Major Noel Morgan-Davies and HQ Company under Major John Cameron-Davies.

In the early stages of 2RAR's formation, such companies were deployed independently where the need arose and not necessarily under their own battalion command. Fortunately, this was not always the case. Later on, and whenever possible, 2RAR companies were deployed into the Chiredzi area under their own battalion command and control which, on occasion, included external cross-border operations into Mozambique.

When companies concluded their operational stint, usually of six-week duration, followed by ten days so called rest and recuperation, they returned to the showgrounds at Fort Victoria where they were housed in makeshift accommodation in tents or various showgrounds buildings. A new barracks for 2RAR was under construction in Fort Victoria. A Company was to become the first occupants in December 1976, with other companies following as the buildings were constructed. After much discussion and suggestions from allcomers, the new barracks was called 'Masvingo', which was subsequently to become the new name for Fort Victoria itself.

In April 1977, Lieutenant-Colonel Peter Hosking was promoted on transfer to Army Headquarters, and in May 1977 Lieutenant-Colonel John McVey took over command of 2RAR, which was still continuously deployed on operations. It was in mid-1977 that the Battalion Tactical HQ was deployed to Grand Reef airfield near Umtali.

In June 1978, 2RAR second-in-command, Major Ian Pullar, was promoted to lieutenant-colonel and given command of the Battalion, which was again redeployed back to its old stomping grounds in the Victoria Province under the command of JOC *Repulse*.

2RAR started a new tactic on 20 June 1978, whereby the Battalion Tactical HQ, together with a full Fire Force, deployed quite openly in the farming areas in the south-eastern area. The battalion managed to field, in addition to the Fire Force, two complete companies and often even three companies, under its own command. The troops would walk in by night in small groups, covering a very wide area and establishing observation positions. These positions were, in the main, based on information provided by the police Special Branch. (SB). This proved an effective tactic in terms of contacts, kills and captures, but overall it wasn't going to win the war.

The areas which were invested by 2RAR during this period covered Devuli Ranch, Great Zimbabwe, Palm River, Chiredzi, Bolo Ranch, Glenclova, Glenlivet, Mkwasine, Rutenga, Mashaba and Nuanetsi. This was over a period of seven months, during which the operations achieved considerable success.

Continuous operations rarely gave an opportunity of getting the whole unit together for dinners, photos, and other such non-operational activities, because by this stage operational demands were steadily increasing. In early 1979, Lieutenant-Colonel Pullar, having spent three years with 2RAR, was transferred and replaced by Lieutenant-Colonel Terry Hammond.

At this stage, majority rule elections had been held and a new Government of National Unity had been formed. The country now became Zimbabwe-Rhodesia, with the first black prime minister, Bishop Abel Muzorewa. Meanwhile the war and operations escalated.

Regrettably, one of the many casualties at this time, was the death in action of 2RAR's first company commander, Major André Dennison MLM, BCR, on 3 June 1979.

On 6 October 1979, 2RAR was granted the Freedom of the Municipality of Fort Victoria and having paraded the scroll, marched through the city for the very first formal parade of the entire battalion.

After Independence in 1980, 2RAR settled into its new barracks in the city, a welcome break from operations.

Company officers commanding in the short but worthy life of 2nd Battalion RAR, included:

A Company:	Major André Dennison
B Company:	Major John Pritchard; Major Colin Hendrie
C Company:	Major Nick Fawcett; Captain Paul Hopcroft
D Company:	Major Noel Morgan-Davies; Major Brian McDermott
HQ Company:	Captain then Major John Cameron-Davies
Support Company:	Major Noel Morgan-Davies

Training Wing 1RAR was committed to training recruits for both 1RAR and 2RAR. This was unsatisfactory, as Methuen Barracks was bursting at the seams. However, authority was granted for a regimental depot to be formed in 1975. Initially this was to be sited next to Methuen Barracks, but before construction started, the decision was made to purchase St Stephen's College, Balla Balla, as this school had been closed down.

The depot opened at Balla Balla on 1 January 1976. The first course of 250 recruits began that week. In addition to recruit training, Depot was responsible for all regimental courses. The first passing-out parade of recruits at Depot RAR took place on 2 July 1976, coinciding with Depot being named Shaw Barracks, after the late chief of staff, Major-General John Shaw DCD, who died tragically in a helicopter crash shortly before Christmas 1975.

Operations *Thrasher* and *Repulse* were created as a renewed terrorist offensive against Rhodesia's eastern and south-eastern border regions began in earnest in January 1976. A and B Companies, 2RAR ,were both committed, in addition to 1RAR, which continued to be mainly deployed in Operation *Hurricane*.

A recommendation for a standardized establishment of an African battalion submitted by the 1st Battalion in February 1975, was approved on 1 April 1976. As a result, E Company 1RAR was transferred to 2RAR as C Company of that unit. The company had been formed in 1965 and had had an illustrious career. The establishment of a fifth rifle company was one of the unique peculiarities of 1RAR. It was fitting that E Company transferred as an entity and not disbanded all together.

The new establishment had four rifle companies, whilst Support Company in the 1st Battalion had 81mm and 60mm mortar, tracker/recce, anti-tank, and assault pioneer platoons. At this time, the anti-tank platoon's weapons had not been finalized, but they were later to receive 106mm recoilless anti-tank rifles.

From 1 January 1976, 1RAR operated from JOC Mtoko, where it accounted for 133 terrorists killed and forty-five captured. The battalion could not boast all the glory, but certainly claimed the majority of the successes. Security force casualties were only twelve killed and 155 wounded. Of this figure, landmines accounted for one killed and 120 injured.

After so many years away from the 1 Brigade area, 1RAR made many representations to move back to HQ, 1 Brigade, Bulawayo.

Eventually in March 1977, 1RAR returned to fall under command of 1 Brigade, with battalion HQ deployed to Fort Victoria. 1 Brigade, besides commanding Operation *Tangent* from Bulawayo, it also commanded Operation *Repulse* in the south-eastern Victoria Province. This meant that instead of a nine-hour drive to Mtoko, it was only a three-hour drive to Fort Victoria. The battalion operated in Victoria, Gutu, Bikita, Zaka, Chibi, Shabani and Belingwe districts. One company was always detached to Op *Tangent*, and based in Gwanda at that time. During 1976 and 1977, the 1st Battalion scored some notable successes against the enemy, both internally and in Mozambique.

At this time, it was recognized by many that the majority of RAR troops now had over ten years' operational service. RAR officers, as always, continued to fight for improved conditions of service and pay for AS (African soldiers).

In late 1977, to increase the regular component of the army and ease the demands on territorial members, the Independent Companies became 'Independent RAR Companies'. National service troops were sent to the territorial battalions and RAR-badged. At the same time, African soldiers were also posted to the territorial Rhodesia Regiment battalions.

In January 1977, a Canberra bomber was shot down over Mozambique and elements of 1RAR were sent in to clear the wreckage. During 1976 and 1977, 2RAR was almost fully established as regards manpower, with shortfalls of thirty-four in Support Company and ninety-nine in HQ Company.

At this time it was the intention of Army HQ to double the number of rifle companies in both 1 and 2RAR with a view to the formation of other battalions. 2RAR was responsible for sub-JOC Umtali, Grand Reef, for ten months during 1977. There were usually at least two companies under the command of sub-JOC Umtali; the other companies were in the Operation *Hurricane* area.

In addition, companies did occasional stints as Fire Force at Grand Reef. All the companies had successes in the operational area:

	Killed	Captured
A Company	77	10
B Company	48	15
C Company	140	15
D Company	70	4
Support Company	17	2

During the same period, 2RAR had one officer and nine other ranks killed.

Two companies, namely B and D, had at least one platoon of men trained in parachuting. These platoons were used as the para-element of the Fire Force, with considerable success. It was hoped in time to have one platoon in each company para-trained.

3RAR began forming in 1977 and 4RAR in 1978.

In June 1977, the first black officers were commissioned at the School of Infantry in Gwelo. Lieutenant Martin Tumbare DMM, received Lieutenant-Colonel Kim Rule's sword from Mrs Rule, on being the first commissioned African officer in the RAR.

After a few months in Fort Victoria, 1RAR moved to Wankie on 11 November 1977 for seven months. On 9 June, the battalion was relieved of its sub-JOC responsibilities and sent on a roving mission within Matabeleland. Between 9 June and 31 August, 1RAR established its main HQ in five different locations. Coincidentally, every time the brigade commander visited the battalion in the field it moved the next day. Following his third visit, the various group commanders reported that they were packed and ready and wanted to know the destination and timings.

The concept of superimposing the regular battalions in a mobile role on to the more active areas, had one advantage for the battalion, and that was that it could operate as a battalion (less one company) under Battalion HQ 1RAR, and without other appendages. The battalion had not had this since mid-1974.

In August 1977, COMOPS came up with another plan. 1RAR would operate as a complete battalion, composed of four rifle companies and Support Company, all under Battalion HQ. 1RAR would man its own Fire Force with helicopters and para Dakota. All great news, but then came the crunch. 1RAR was to return to under the command of JOC *Hurricane*.

Successes continued internally and externally.

During this period, one of Support Company's recce/ambush patrols had a contact with four CTs, wounding and capturing the logistics officer who had prepared a crossing for ninety CTs. The patrol then set an ambush for that night, but nothing happened. As they started to dismantle the ambush the next morning, seventy CTs came down the pathway. The patrol squirmed back under the sparse cover and waited. Spread out as they were, everybody waited for the platoon commander, Lt Pat Lawless to spring the ambush. At least eight CTs were killed and some ten to fifteen wounded in the initial firefight. Unknown to the patrol, another twenty CTs tried to outflank them, coming down a hillock onto their rear. One soldier saw this move and charged the CTs. He killed two, threw a grenade at the remainder and dispersed the CTs.

In 1978, the first RAR troops were sent for paratroop training and were thereafter actively involved in Fire Force operations. Rhodesian paratroops jumped from minimum heights, and in fact RAR probably held the record, as a stick commanded by Lieutenant 'Blackie' Swart jumped and hit the ground only as their 'chutes began to deploy. The entire stick had to be casevaced but luckily, none of the members sustained fatal injuries.

During this period, A Company was detached for about three months on Fire Force duties at Mtoko, where they had great success and, together with the air force, accounted for ninety-four CTs.

At this time, 1RAR had 126 trained paratroopers. This was to increase to 200 by December of 1978. One soldier was killed in a million-to-one chance accident during a training jump. A sad day, but the African soldiers loved parachuting and were proud of their new-found ability.

Much of 1978 and 1979 was spent in the Op *Hurricane* area and included a number of external operations, some in support of the Selous Scouts and the SAS.

It was in August 1979 that the battalion was committed to training the Security Force Auxiliaries (SFA). Thus the year was not as active as in previous years, as it was spent training and later controlling the SFA. The battalion did not enjoy this on the whole, because it was slow-moving and frustrating, and the battalion was spread by companies under command of various sub-JOCs. It was considered that by the end of 1979 the SFA had started to earn their pay and a proportion of the credit for getting the SFA to that standard was due to the officers and men within the companies. The whole exercise was a good illustration of RAR versatility.

From the SFA, the battalion moved on, as a battalion, to the Matabeleland North area of operations, where it was soon back in the swing of things both internally and externally. External operations included a very successful operation in the Kabanga Mission area.

Operation *Murex*, as it was to be called, was a combined Fire Force and ground operation from Wankie FAF. The aim of the mission was to cut ZIPRA communications with the terrorists operating in Rhodesia. The target was a conventionally trained battalion of ZIPRA CTs defending an area of open ground two to three kilometres square, covered with anthills 100 metres apart, each being defended by at least one section. The camp was dug in northwest of Kabanga Mission. On 4 November 1979, Support Company, 1RAR, which included sixteen paratroopers from the battalion and eighteen from the Selous Scouts, attacked an enemy base. In support were two DC-3 'Dakota' transporters; six Agusta Bell 205 'Cheetah' helicopters; four Alouette III command and gunship 'K-car' helicopters; six Alouette III 'G-car' troop helicopters armed with machine guns; Canberra bombers; and Hawker Hunters were used to open the attack. One Selous Scout was killed in the action, but at least 100 ZIPRA regulars were killed and many wounded. One prisoner was taken and huge quantities of equipment captured or destroyed, including a communications bunker. The raid ended on 5 November 1979 at 1000 in the morning. The Cheetahs were used to take out the troops while the G-cars and K-cars covered the withdrawal. Two G-cars were hit in the raid, but this was only discovered on the return to the Deka airstrip.

Peace then came with a ceasefire. 1RAR was redeployed to fall under the command of 4 Brigade, in an attempt to curb the rampant intimidation going on in the run-up to the Zimbabwe independence elections. From March 1980 onwards, 1RAR operated out of Methuen Barracks, with companies going off for exercises, battle camps and adventure training.

In mid-1980, 2RAR took part in what was to be one of the largest recorded classical war exercises ever carried out by Rhodesian army units. The exercise included 2RAR and support elements of 1RAR, including the 1RAR Tac HQ vehicle (2.5 MAP), A Troop and B Troop of P Battery, Rhodesian Artillery, and armoured cars and T-54 tanks of the Rhodesian Armoured Cars Regiment. From the air force, Hawker Hunter jets and 'Lynx' aircraft participated. School of Infantry regular officer cadets took part as well.

On 18 April 1980, 1RAR provided the guard of honour for the farewell of His Royal Highness, The Prince of Wales, and Lord Christopher Soames. The Prince of Wales inspected the colour party, guard of honour and regimental band.

Prince Charles had visited the RAR before leaving the country, where he signed the drum skin which can now be seen in the Rifles Officers' Club in London (See Appendix IV).

3rd Battalion and Independent Companies

Political and military pressures intensified on Rhodesia during the period from 1975 to 1978. The internal settlement, the Kissinger 'shuttle diplomacy', and on-going fruitless talks to try to persuade the Patriotic Front to work with Ian Smith's Rhodesia Front party, had a negative effect on the remaining whites who formed the backbone of the territorial force army.

As they left the country, more and greater gaps appeared in the conscript battalions and national service independent companies. National service was extended to include young blacks for the first time, while low-calibre surrendered terrorists were armed and formed into auxiliary units in an effort to bolster the weakening front line.

Another solution was the formation of a third RAR battalion. Fortunately, the outline structure of a battalion was already in existence. The oft-maligned staff in Army Headquarters devised a plan, which embodied the best of innovation and resource in order to launch the 3rd Battalion as rapidly as possible.

Spread about the Rhodesian borders were six independent companies of the territorial Rhodesia Regiment. These units were initially manned by young white school leavers, and had been giving a good account of themselves for a number of years. A happy coincidence placed 5 and 6 (Indep) Companies in the same barracks in Umtali (now Mutare).

Not far away to the north, at the newly built Inyanga Barracks, was based 3 (Indep) Company. Chipinga, an important farming area to the south of Umtali, had a company base and all the back-up infrastructure sited next to the airfield. In 1978, the responsibility for providing a credible military force in the Chipinga area was moved from a territorial force battalion, the 10th Battalion, The Rhodesia Regiment, to 5 and 6 (Indep) Companies, which rotated on a six-week changeover basis.

At this time, several platoons of young black conscripts, sent to bolster the ranks of the local citizen force battalion, the 4th (Manicaland) Battalion, The Rhodesia Regiment, were put under the command of the officers commanding 5 and 6 (Indep) Companies for administrative purposes, because there was no on-going capability to do this in the 4th Battalion. They effectively became a third independent company, and because of the increasing numbers of black troops coming into the independent companies, these were now badged 'RAR' instead of 'RR'.

A consequence of all this evolution was that the Umtali independent companies were, in effect, another battalion of the RAR. Army HQ began to post in senior NCOs from the 1st and 2nd Battalions. A number of courses were run at Balla Balla (Depot, RAR), to inculcate the values and traditions required of RAR soldiers into the Umtali and Inyanga troops.

It was fortunate that the facilities of Addams Barracks, the original home of 5 and 6 (Indep) Companies were excellent. Addams Barracks had been named after a well-known and highly respected son of Umtali, Major Ernest 'Doomps' Addams, killed at a contact site near Madziwa on 14 August 1974. His son, as a national service sergeant, came to 5 (Indep) Coy, RR, in 1978. The site had formerly been a private school, which had been forced by the war to close down. With minimal refurbishing and some minor adjustments, the barracks became an admirable battalion base. By mid-1979, the troops occupying this building knew that they were to become 3RAR. A new sense of purpose swept through the barracks.

In September of 1979, it was announced that 3RAR would be formed early in 1980. Immediately, Army HQ began posting staff and vehicles, and weapons and equipment in anticipation of the event. The independent companies became A, B, C and D Companies, and allocated commanders as follows:

A Company	Major Tom Simpson
B Company	Major Marius Meiring
C Company	Major Euan Cormack-Thompson
D Company	Major Frederick Freiherr von der Trenck
HQ Company	Major Jim Flanagan
Adjutant	Captain T.L. Hughes
Quartermaster	Lieutenant N.W.C. Boardman
MTO	Lieutenant D.J. Famden
RSM	Warrant Officer Class I C. Veremu
RQMS	Warrant Officer Class I G. Byrne

Lieutenants Fuyane and Gomba, two of the army's earliest commissioned black officers, were appointed seconds-in-command of C and D Companies respectively.

Acting Lieutenant-Colonel Terry Leaver was appointed CO designate in October 1979. Lord Christopher Soames, the transient governor of Southern Rhodesia, was eventually to sign the warrant to enable the battalion to formally come into existence on 1 March 1980. However, the unit was already a *de facto* entity.

In the early days, Captain Rory Downey, a territorial force officer, provided additional officer support to whichever company deployed to Chipinga or Inyanga. Major Euan Cormack-Thompson doubled as battalion second-in-command. Squadron Leader Don Howe, a legendary figure in the Rhodesian Air Force, as well as being one of the few remaining veterans of the Battle of Britain to still be in uniform, came to the new battalion as captain to be admin officer and camp commandant.

Finally, yet importantly, the battalion inherited Staff Sergeant 'Siggy' Sigurdsson from Iceland, whose cordon bleu qualifications served the unit well in both base and field kitchens. They were, however, unable to use Siggy's other qualification as a pilot, having neither DC3s nor Bell HU-l (Huey) helicopters on their inventory. Siggy had come to Rhodesia hoping to join the Rhodesian Air Force, but when his command of English failed to meet the 'Blues' requirements, the battalion was very glad to use his back-up qualification

Rory Downey's contribution to the battalion was considerable. A management consultant, who had experience on a global basis, he was one of the few who returned to Rhodesia when the war became tough, volunteering his services on the condition that he would be in an operational unit, not a 'pen-pusher'. Major-General A.N.O. 'Derry' MacIntyre OLM, DCD had first used Rory to conduct investigations into several of the army's logistical procedures, and thereafter he came to serve in 6 (Indep) Company and 3RAR where his sense of humour, great competence and willingness to go where the fighting was, endeared him to all. His management skills and vision contributed in no small way to the smoothness of 3RAR's formation.

3RAR, whilst not officially a promulgated unit, commenced operating as a battalion from the end of October, 1979. At this stage, the Lancaster House Conference was in the middle of its negotiations. Infiltration from across the Mozambique border was a serious concern, as Mugabe's forces jockeyed for strength with the Rhodesians, hoping to gain ground both physically and in the consultations in London.

The unit was constantly in the field, from the northern Inyanga area through to Cashel and Chimanimani regions. Sporadic contacts occurred. There were two kills in the Inyanga area when the CO designate and Second Lieutenant Pretorius were dropped from a command helicopter returning to Inyanga to refuel, after the pilot spotted suspicious movements.

In December 1979, in accordance with the terms agreed in the Lancaster House Agreement, Lord Soames arrived to fulfil the role of governor of the country until the result of the forthcoming election was known. Throughout this time, the combined forces of ZANLA and ZIPRA, known now as the Patriotic Front, were to be confined in previously agreed 'assembly points' under the control of the Monitoring Force, drawn from countries around the world, including Britain, Australia, Fiji and Nigeria.

Assembly Point "Foxtrot', the largest of them, was in Buhera district, in the western area of 3RAR's jurisdiction. Battalion HQ and a company deployed to Buhera village, whilst the remainder of the Battalion deployed to their normal spheres of operations in Inyanga, Chipinga, Umtali, Melsetter and Mount Selinda.

The end

On 4 March 1980, the outcome of the Zimbabwe independence elections swept Robert Mugabe and his ZANU (PF) party to power with an overwhelming majority. HRH Prince Charles represented the Crown at the handover ceremony, and as he and Lord Soames left the newly independent Zimbabwe, elements of 1RAR provided the guard of honour.

On 23 April that year, the 4th Battalion (Holding Unit) the Rhodesian African Rifles, was formed, primarily to absorb the Selous Scouts, the latter immediately disbanded by the new government. Former members of the SAS and the RLI also asked to be transferred to this unit. Initially commanded by Major Dudley Coventry (SAS), the battalion would wear the identical embellishments as the other three RAR battalions. He assumed second-in-command when Lieutenant-Colonel Brian Robinson (SAS) became commanding officer. The life of this battalion was short-lived however, as on 1 October 1980 it became the 1st Zimbabwe Parachute Battalion.

In spite of the end of the bush war, tensions between the erstwhile partners in the fight for the country's freedom remained high, particularly in Entumbane, a large, heavily populated African township northwest of Bulawayo.

In November 1980, 3,000 ZIPRA and an equal number of ZANLA cadres were moved from their respective assembly points into temporary accommodation in Entumbane, there to await integration into the fledgling Zimbabwe National Army. This move was ill-conceived, as the two factions had a long-standing dislike of the each other, a relationship which, arguably, goes back to the days of Lobengula when the amaNdebele had effectively enslaved the chiShona-speaking ethnic groups in that part of southern Africa.

Fighting inevitably erupted on 8 November, as the opposing groups used all their guerrilla weaponry and ordnance in an attempt to eliminate the other. 1RAR, although now renamed the 11th Infantry Battalion but still wearing their Rhodesian uniforms, badges and embellishments, was deployed to defuse the situation. A, B, C, D and Support Companies provided an extended barrier to protect the city, but late that night relative calm returned, broken only periodically by isolated shooting. The hospitals were swamped with wounded civilians caught up in the fighting.

As the antagonists dug in during the night, the embattled ZIPRA called in a ZIPRA motorised infantry brigade from its assembly point at Gwaai River Mine. On arrival at Entumbane at first light, the unit erected roadblocks, at the same time launching a full-blown attack on ZANLA positions. The RAR troops, up until now under orders not to use force, were given the go ahead to intervene. D Company was positioned, with extra machine guns, at a beer hall overlooking the two guerrilla camps. It is believed that the presence of the RAR troops, led by white officers, was the cause of a cessation of firing by the two factions. Acting on advice from the commander of 1 Brigade, Brigadier (later Major-General) Mike Shute OLM, with senior guerrilla commanders Rex Nhongo (ZANLA) and Dumiso Dabengwa (ZIPRA), brokered a ceasefire. On-going resentment of the proximity of the other faction ensured that peace was tenuous. Heavily armed elements of 1RAR remained deployed at the beer hall.

By the beginning of 1981, it was becoming abundantly clear to Joshua Nkomo and his ZAPU party that the new regime would not entertain any thoughts of power-sharing, and ZIPRA started increasing its strength in Matabeleland. This included bolstering the force at Gwaai River Mine to include armoured personnel carriers and tanks. At this time, the only regular infantry troops were 1RAR under Lieutenant-Colonel 'Mick' McKenna.

McKenna, identifying Entumbane as the most probable flash point, made the beer hall the main operational base, and in so doing, significantly fortified the position. Company commanders dubbed the base 'Rorke's Drift' or 'The Alamo'. Concerned that a fresh outbreak of fighting between the two factions would result in further ZIPRA reinforcements arriving from Gwaai River Mine, McKenna set up four-man OP teams on the main roads leading into Bulawayo, especially those from Victoria Falls and Essexvale.

On 8 February, ZANLA guerrillas attacked ZIPRA camp at Connemara in the Midlands, inflicting heavy casualties. When news of this reached ZIPRA elements in the new 13 Infantry Battalion east of Entumbane, they overran a ZANLA position, inflicting heavy casualties. McKenna sent in D Company under American Lieutenant Dave Hill to restore order. Taking with him a squadron of four Eland-90 armoured cars, commanded by Sergeant

'Skippy' Devine, Hill and his men neutralized the ZIPRA position, literally flattening the camp tents with their armoured cars. Forty ZIPRA guerrillas were killed.

Three days later, C Company commander, Major Lionel Dyck, reported a massive increase in activity in the ZIPRA camp. Ordered not to become involved, Dyck immediately set about preparing 'The Alamo' for an attack, positioning the twenty-four MAGs at his disposal in six sectors with four MAGs in each.

At eight o'clock that night, a major fight commenced as the two factions not only threw everything they had at each other, but also started attacking the RAR base. As small-arms fire raked the base and 60mm and 82mm mortars crashed around them, Dyck was ordered to withdraw – an instruction clearly impossible to execute.

A short while later, McKenna reacted to an OP sighting of a ZIPRA column approaching Bulawayo from Essexvale (now Esigodini) by deploying Devine and his Elands to the suburban outskirts of Bulawayo to intercept. In a successful series of engagements, Devine accounted for several ZIPRA BTR-152 armoured personnel carriers, inflicting significant casualties.

At 'The Alamo', however, the situation was critical for the men of C Company. ZIPRA, having successfully routed the ZANLA combatants, turned their full attention to the RAR base. A propeller-driven adapted ground-attack aircraft developed by the Rhodesians during the war and named a 'Lynx', conducted several sorties under concentrated ground fire against the ZIPRA assailants. With mortars now exploding inside the base, the situation was desperate for Dyck, but they held on until one o'clock the following afternoon when a relief column made up of B and D companies arrived at 'The Alamo'. Major Dyck was awarded the Silver Cross of Zimbabwe for his brave actions in the successful defence of his base.

In April 1981, the Rhodesian African Rifles celebrated its final Regimental Week, in memory of the 1RAR victory over the Japanese at Tanlwe Chaung during the Second World War. In a private ceremony, the battalion beat the retreat for the last time, and with immense pride in its sixty-five year history, *Sweet Banana* was sung for the last time and the Colours laid-up.

1st Battalion Rhodesian African Rifles Officers and European NCOs , c. 1948. Back row: Bill Curnow-Baker, Frank Sinclair, Tony Coppinger, Derek de Villiers, Peter Henwood, Tickey McLoughlin, Don Campbell-Morrison. Middle row: Jock Campbell, Bob Prentice, Benney Baxter, Spike Lachenicht, Jerry Took, Pop Brimms (bandmaster), RSM Fred Cookes, Ted Cutter, Bill Boyd, Ian Grimmer. Front row: Lt Mick Kemp, Lt Wally Belton, Capt Jimmy Young, Maj Kim Rule, Lt-Col Tommy Walls, Capt Guy Bain, Lt Paddy Dooge, Lt Benny Franklin.

Top left: 1RAR troops boarding transport on the way to the docks in Mombasa, 2 December 1944.

Above: C Coy 1RAR burn a Japanese basha camp in the Pegu Yomas 1945.

Far left: On the Taungoo to Mawchi road with A Coy in 1945.

Left: 1RAR troops crossing a ravine on a temporary bridge in the Arakan.

C Coy 1RAR officers at Waw, Burma January 1946. From left: Jimmy Wright, Bernard Burton, John English, Mike Hagelthorn, Bill Ferris and Steve Davies (OC).

Victory Parade in London. The Southern Rhodesia Contingent march past King George VI. The two escorts to the Southern Rhodesian Colour are sergeants in the RAR.

HM King George VI inspects the 1RAR Guard of Honour on his visit to Rhodesia in1947. The Guard Commander is Maj G.E.L.Rule.

1RAR Officers at the Ikwani Training Camp. From left: Frank Fitzgerald, Curly Radford, Guy Bain, Jenks Jenkins, Peter Walls, Benny Franklin, Maurice Wheaton, Paddy Douge and Don Campbell-Morrison.

An RAR Regimental Association function 1950. In front Maj Walker (2ic 1RAR Burma). Seated: Col Ferris (LO WW2), Lt-Col F.J.Wane ISO (first CO) and Lt-Col Kim Rule (CO). Seated on left: Reg Spitteler and Reg Lowings. Seated on the right :Guy Bain. Front row standing: Stan Morris, unknown, Allen, George Hartley, G.Francis, Benny Baxter, unknown, Steve Comberbach, unknown, Geoff Betts and Bowles. Back row standing: unknown, C.D.Coventry, George Pitt, Clarry Adams and Denis Divaris.

General Sir John Harding GCB, CBE, DSO & Two Bars, MC meets some of the African NCOs. Here he is shaking hands with CSM Chimwe of A Coy.

Some of the officers on their return from Egypt. From left: Lt Bill de Haast, Lt J.R. Fayrer-Hoskin, Capt George Pitt MC, Maj Wally Belton (OC) and Capt Paddy Dooge.

A Company 1RAR training with the 3rd Battalion the Coldstream Guards in Egypt. Standing: CSM de Villiers, a Coldstream Guards instructor and Sgt Crookes. Kneeling: Sgt Taruberakera, Sgt Nkatazo, Sgt Bobo and CSM Chimwe.

1RAR members who went to the 1953 Coronation with the Southern Rhodesia Contingent. From left: CSM Hassan, CSM Takarusa, RSM Elijah and CSM Chimwe.

RSM Elijah in the UK with the Coronation Contingent.

Lieutenant-Colonel G.E.L. 'Kim' Rule OBE retired. One of the most influential commanding officers that the RAR had in its short history.

Her Majesty Queen Elizabeth the Queen Mother presents the Royal Colour to Lt M Pillar before moving over to present the Regimental Colour to Lt O.M.Atkinson.

The Chaplain-General, the Rt Revd E.F.Paget CBE, MC, DD consecrates the Colours at the Drumhead Service.

Members of 8 Platoon training for Malaya.

'O Group'. From left: Sergeant Gondocondo, Lance-Corporal Kephas, Corporal Taderera and Cpl Tabuya.

L Cpl Muchembere gives orders to his Bren gun team.

Askari preparing to disembark on the home bank. Captain Bill Curnow-Baker is in the stern of the loaded inflatable

A patrol near the jungle edge moving through a patch of *lallang* (grass) and *belukar* (giant, sharp fern).

Platoon Warrant Officer Pisayi Muzerecho MM and Sergeant Gondocondo at their evening meal. Malayan Emergency 1956–58.

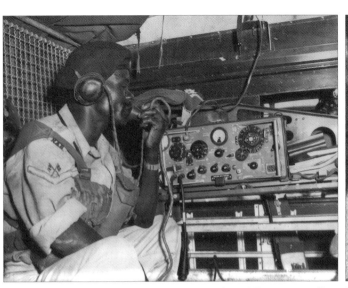

Nyasaland Emergency. L Cpl Thinkwell and fellow troops conduct a cordon and search at Mikilongwe, a hotbed of ANC agitation in the Southern province.

L Cpl Thinkwell in the CO's command Land Rover sending a message on his 62 radio set.

Lt Nick Smith A Coy 1RAR killed in action with CSM Timitiya 22 August 1967 during Op *Nickle*.

Op *Grampus*, near Binga. Six captured terrorists kneeling in front of PWO Wurayayi's patrol. Wurayayi was awarded the BCR for his conduct.

An overjoyed warrant officer holds his infant son for the first time.

The Mayoress of Bulawayo, Mrs Menashe, presents L Cpl Tavashure with the Malvern Cup, after winning the army knock-out cup for the third time. Battalion football officer, Maj David Heppenstall looks on.

Op *Grampus*. 11 Pl D Coy 1RAR move in on the enemy in Devil's Gorge.

Lt A.K.Tourle BCR, Lt R.Marillier BCR, Brig Reg Edwards DSO, MC (Reviewing Officer), Maj J.R.Wells-West (2ic 1RAR) and Cpl Kenias Tovakare BCR.

Mascot L Cpl Induna kneeling, looking over two prospective mascot recruits, Tendai and Zwanamina, gifts from Senator Chief Kayisa.

The honorary colonel with a group of RAR WOs. From left: Colonel C.B.McCullagh MBE, RSM, N. Tumbare, CSM Obert Veremu, CSM Pfupa, CSM Gobe, CSM Kisi and CSM Kephasi.

The Mayor of Salisbury, Councillor Tanser, and Maurice Mills, Chairman of the RAR Regimental Association, unveil the commemorative plaque on the site of the old RAR camp on the Borrowdale Road.

Prime Minister Ian Smith visits 1RAR on *Op Hurricane* at the Battalion HQ at Sipolilo. Here he is chatting to CSM Marambanyika of C Coy.

PWO Gibson Mugadza BCR and Pte Phinias Foshore BCR talking to President Clifford Dupont ID and Minister of Defence P.K. van der Byl ID.

Admiral Bierman (Commander SADF) signs the Regimental drumskin at Methuen Barracks when the town adopted the Battalion. Looking on are Lt-Col Barnard DCD (CO 1RAR) and P.W.Botha (SA Minister of Defence).

1RAR detachments march on parade in Sinoia, 1975.

President, John Wrathall presents CSM Yangama Kupara with his BCR for outstanding leadership and bravery in action.

2Lt Andy Telfer SCR.

The President congratulates WOII V. Rashayi on his award of the BCR.

Mrs Rule, the widow of Lt-Col Kim Rule OBE, presents her late husband's sword to the first African to be commissioned, Lt N.M.Tumbare DMM.

Right: John Wrathall presents Maj André Dennison with his MLM.

Far right: Maj Nick Fawcett after receiving his OLM from the President.

Farewell to Maj Bandy Macdonald. Dining Out Night Llewellin Bks 1RAR Officers' Mess. Lt-Col Terry Hammond (2RAR), Lt-Col Mick McKenna (CO 1RAR), Maj Bandy Macdonald and Lt-Col Ian Bate (1RLI).

Cpl Matafeni and L Cpl Moswa on patrol during the bush war of the 1970s.

Fire Force Paratroopers A Coy 2RAR line up for inspection and checking of equipment.

A Company 2RAR 'Heavies' ready for action.

2Lt Graeme Trass receives his SCR from the Army Commander Maj-Gen A.L.C. 'Sandy' Maclean.

L Cpl Raymond Hariori is presented with his SCR.

Cpl Ananias Ali is presented with the SCR.

The Army Commander presents Cpl Calvin Ncube with his BCR.

2Lt Chris Vincent is presented with his BCR.

Pte George Mponda BCR.

L Cpl Henry Mawire BCR

Time for a quick smoke, and then get ready for the next one.

Relief and smiles as all come back safely after a job well done.

2RAR receive the Freedom of Fort Victoria, 1979.

'I'll be pleased to put this potent weapon down for a bit.'

Bush patrol.

1RAR platoon on the approach march 1976.

1RAR march past the mayor of Bulawayo, Tanlwe Chaung Day, 1976.

Chapter 3

Roll of Honour: RNR WWI

Surname	Name	Number	Rank	Status	DoD	Footnote
Adamu		M1631	Pte	DOAS	09/12/1918	Died of pneumonia at Ntondwe, Nyasaland. Source: NAZ.
Aiedi		M1830	Pte	DOAS	14/11/1917	Source: *Masodja*. Listed on the Harare Memorial in the Pioneer Cemetery. Source: CWGC.
Ali		3941	N Cst	DOAS	05/12/1918	Died of pneumonia at Ntondwe, Nyasaland. From BSAP. Source: NAZ.
Alick		M151	Cpl	DOAS	23/10/1918	Died of unknown cause. Source: NAZ and *Masodja*. Listed on the Harare Memorial in the Pioneer Cemetery. Source: CWGC.
Alunanda		M66	Pte	MIA	23/03/1917	Missing believed dead. Source: NAZ.
Amanda		M1433	Pte	DOAS	27/12/1918	Died of pneumonia at Ntondwe, Nyasaland. Source: NAZ.
Amlani		M109	Pte	DOAS	10/04/1917	Died from dysentery at Zomba, Nyasaland. Source: NAZ and *Masodja*.
Amundala		M1879	Pte	DOAS	01/12/1918	Died of pneumonia at Ntondwe, Nyasaland. Source: NAZ.
Anderson	Augustus Eric Hugh	1264	S Sgt	KIA	20/03/1917	Born in Newcastle, Natal, he died at the age of 26 years. Ex-BSAP Sinoia (No. 1264, attest: 23 Jul 1910). He is buried in the Iringa Cemetery, Tanzania. Source: CWGC, NAZ and *Masodja*.
Bageli	Kleinboi	M988	Pte	DOAS	05/12/1918	Died of pneumonia at Ntondwe, Nyasaland. Source: NAZ.
Baker	William James	Not issued	T Capt	KIA	29/03/1917	Died of wounds aged 37 years. Born in London, England, he is buried in Iringa Cemetery, Tanzania. Awarded the *Croix de Guere* (France) and Mentioned in Despatches. Source: CWGC, NAZ and *Masodja*.
Basaboy		M1684	Pte	DOAS	08/08/1918	Died of unknown cause. Source: NAZ.
Bendi		M832	Pte	DOAS	31/05/1917	Died of unknown cause. Source: NAZ and Masodja. Listed on the Harare Memorial in the Pioneer Cemetery. Source: CWGC.
Bidu		M271	Pte	KIA	23/10/1916	Source: NAZ.
Boma		M748	Pte	DOAS	26/11/1917	Died of pneumonia at Limbe, Nyasaland. DoD also listed as 24 November. Source: NAZ and *Masodja*.
Bridges	Eric Forster	Not issued	Lt	KIA	29/01/1917	Died from wounds, aged 29 years. He is buried in the Iringa Cemetery in Tanzania. Also served with 1RR and the BSAP (No. 928 attest: 23 Oct 1907). Source: CWGC, NAZ and *Masodja*.
Burke	Frederick Charles		Sgt	KIA	18/10/1918	Wounded in action 29 Jan 1917. Ex-BSAP Capt., Salisbury (No. 137, attest: 26 May 1905). Source: NAZ.
Bwanali		M112	Pte	MIA	10/11/1916	Missing, presumed killed. Source: NAZ.
Chesayi	Samuel	M2262	Pte	DOAS	30/10/1918	Died of unknown cause. Source: NAZ and *Masodja*. Listed on the Harare Memorial in the Pioneer Cemetery. Source: CWGC.
Chezani		M173	Pte	KIA	29/01/1917	Source: NAZ and *Masodja*.
Chibwana		M488	Pte	KIA	19/08/1917	Killed at Mpepo, GEA (Tanzania). Source: NAZ and *Masodja*.
Chibwana		M1092	Pte	DOAS	18/04/1918	Died of heart failure at Mtengula, Nyasaland. Source: NAZ.
Chibwana		M1802	Pte	DOAS	11/12/1918	Died of pneumonia at Ntondwe, Nyasaland. Source: NAZ and *Masodja*.

Surname	Name	Number	Rank	Status	DoD	Footnote
Chiduro		M1993	Pte	DOAS	12/12/1918	Died of pneumonia at Ntondwe, Nyasaland. Source: NAZ.
Chifapankwa		M1505	Pte	DOAS	26/11/1918	Died of pnuemonia at Limbe, Nyasaland. Source: NAZ.
Chikasawuka		M1128	Pte	DOAS	10/12/1918	Died of pneumonia at Ntondwe, Nyasaland. Source: NAZ.
Chikoko		M1923	Pte	DOAS	11/09/1918	Died of pneumonia at Malokokera. Also spelt Chikoto. Source: NAZ.
Chikombe		M2040	Pte	DOAS	12/12/1918	Died of pneumonia at Ntondwe, Nyasaland. Source: NAZ and *Masodja*.
Chimanga		M1483	Pte	DOAS	21/04/1917	Died of unknown cause. Source: *Masodja*. Listed on the Harare Memorial in the Pioneer Cemetery. Source: CWGC.
Chimbalanga		M237	Pte	KIA	29/01/1917	Source: NAZ and *Masodja*.
Chimkombe			Pte	DOAS	U/K	Died of unknown cause. Source: NAZ.
Chimsoto		M2192	Pte	DOAS	01/06/1918	Died of unknown cause. Source: NAZ and *Masodja*. Listed on the Harare Memorial in the Pioneer Cemetery. Source: CWGC.
Chimwasi		M1982	L Cpl	DOAS	U/K	Died of unknown cause. Source: NAZ.
Chindoko		M1410	Pte	DOAS	U/K	Died of unknown cause. Source: NAZ.
Chunduro			Pte	DOAS	U/K	Died of unknown cause. Source: NAZ.
Chinguwa		M1523	Pte	DOAS	03/12/1918	Died of pneumonia at Ntondwe, Nyasaland. Source: NAZ.
Chipeta		M1720	Pte	KOAS	25/07/1918	Died of wounds sustained in an accident at Macubi PEA (Mozambique). Source: NAZ and Masodja.
Chisanga	Johnnie	M1483	Pte	DOAS	21/04/1917	Died of unknown cause. Source: NAZ.
Chitinga		M141	Pte	KIA	23/03/1917	Source: NAZ and *Masodja*.
Chiwa	George	M2220	Pte	DOAS	23/10/1918	Died of unknown cause. Source: NAZ and *Masodja*. Listed on the Harare Memorial in the Pioneer Cemetery. Source: CWGC.
Dafidi		M423	Pte	KIA	30/08/1917	Source: NAZ and *Masodja*.
Danda		M2234	Pte	DOAS	07/11/1918	Died of unknown cause. Source: *Masodja*. Listed on the Harare Memorial in the Pioneer Cemetery. Source: CWGC.
Davite		M1558	Pte	DOAS	03/12/1918	Died of pneumonia at Ntondwe, Nyasaland. Source: NAZ.
Doropa		M2261	Pte	DOAS	U/K	Died of unknown cause. Source: NAZ.
Durrant	Christopher Martin	Not issued	T 2Lt	KOAS	25/07/1918	Accidentally killed in East Africa when a shell exploded prematurely. Ex-BSAP (No. 1952 attest: 18 Aug 1915). Source: NAZ and *Masodja*. Buried in the Lumbo British Cemetery in Mozambique. Source: CWGC.
Duwa		M1881	Pte	DOAS	19/09/1918	Died of pneumonia in East Africa. Source: NAZ.
Fenyoni	Simon	M1219	Pte	DOAS	14/12/1918	Died of pneumonia at Ntondwe, Nyasaland. Source: NAZ.
Fulatela		M1189	Pte	DOAS	09/12/1918	Died of pneumonia at Ntondwe, Nyasaland. Also spelt Fulatele. Source: NAZ and *Masodja*.
Fundusi		3735	N Cst	DOAS	28/10/1918	Died of pneumonia at Beira in PEA (Mozambique). From BSAP. Also spelt Fundasi. Source: NAZ. Buried in the Muhammadan Cemetery in Beira, Mozambique. Source: CWGC.
George		M342	Pte	KIA	17/01/1917	Killed at Songea, GEA (Tanzania). Source: NAZ.

Surname	Name	Number	Rank	Status	DoD	Footnote
Grant	William Bland	MR/32	Sgt	DOAS	11/12/1918	Died of pneumonia at Zomba, Nyasaland, aged 31 years. He is buried in the Zomba Town Cemetery, Malawi. Ex 2RR Private (service number 1623, enlisted 23 May 1916), serving in GEA. Source: CWGC, NAZ, Capell and *Masodja*.
Gwati		M1014	Pte	DOAS	08/12/1918	Died of pneumonia at Ntondwe, Nyasaland. Misspelled as Givati. Source: NAZ and *Masodja*.
Harper	Bertram	Not issued	T 2Lt	DOAS	26/10/1918	Source: NAZ and *Masodja*. Buried in the Pioneer Cemetery, Harare. The CWGC gives his unit as Northern Rhodesia Police. Ex-BSAP (No. 1391 attest: 08 Feb 1911).
Harry	James	M1356	Pte	DOAS	17/12/1918	Died of pneumonia at Ntondwe, Nyasaland. Service number also listed as M1538. Source: NAZ and *Masodja*.
Hlupo		M937	Pte	DOAS	23/11/1917	Died of malaria in GEA (Tanzania). Source: NAZ. Also spelt Hlupa.
Hopkins	F.A.	Not issued	Lt	DOAS	U/K	Awarded the MBE. Source: *Masodja*.
Jama		M1020	Pte	DOAS	11/12/1918	Died of pneumonia at Ntondwe, Nyasaland. Source: NAZ and *Masodja*.
Jamusi		M210	Pte	DOAS	U/K	Died of unknown cause. Source: NAZ.
Jauliji		M184	Pte	KIA	08/11/1916	Died of wounds. Source: NAZ.
John		M178	Pte	DOAS	13/04/1917	Died from exhaustion at Zomba, Nyasaland. Source: NAZ.
Johnathan		M2009	Pte	DOAS	28/10/1918	Died of pneumonia at Ntondwe, Nyasaland. Source: NAZ and *Masodja*. Listed on the Harare Memorial in the Pioneer Cemetery. Source: CWGC.
Kadewa	Julius	M806	Pte	DOAS	17/12/1918	Died of pneumonia at Ntondwe, Nyasaland. Source: NAZ.
Kambani		M1671	Pte	DOAS	08/12/1918	Died of pneumonia at Ntondwe, Nyasaland. Source: NAZ and *Masodja*.
Kamana		M1917	Pte	DOAS	16/06/1918	Died of trypanosomiasis in Port Amelia, PEA (Mozambique). Also spelt Kamwana. Source: NAZ. Listed on the Pemba Memorial in the cemetery in Pemba, Mozambique. Source: CWGC.
Kamwekene		M1704	Pte	DOAS	24/12/1917	Died of heart failure, GEA. Also spelt Kamwekeni (unlikely). Source: NAZ.
Kandawiri		M972	Pte	DOAS	27/02/1918	Died of dysentery at Zomba, Nyasaland. Source: NAZ.
Kanono		M1223	A Cpl	DOAS	U/K	Died of pneumonia at Ntondwe, Nyasaland. Source: NAZ.
Kapakasa		M1712	Pte	DOAS	26/06/1918	Died of dysentery in East Africa. Source: NAZ.
Karumpa		M1957	Pte	DOAS	04/12/1918	Died of pneumonia at Ntondwe, Nyasaland. Source: NAZ.
Kasonda		M1995	Pte	DOAS	22/10/1918	Died of unknown cause. Also spelt Kasondi (unlikely). Source: *Masodja*. Listed on the Harare Memorial in the Pioneer Cemetery. Source: CWGC.
Kauchepa	Marapata	M1572	Pte	DOAS	05/12/1918	Died of pneumonia at Ntondwe, Nyasaland. Source: NAZ.
Kobiri		M369	Pte	KIA	19/08/1917	Source: Was also wounded on 20 Dec 1916. NAZ and *Masodja*.
Komani	Edward	M341	Cpl	DOAS	07/03/1918	Died of tetanus at depot Salisbury. Also listed as wounded. Source: NAZ and *Masodja*. Listed on the Harare Memorial in the Pioneer Cemetery. Source: CWGC.
Komitshi		M1358	Pte	DOAS	12/12/1918	Died of pneumonia at Ntondwe, Nyasaland. Source: NAZ and *Masodja*.
Konde		M2212	Pte	DOAS	11/04/1918	Died of unknown cause. Source: NAZ and *Masodja*. Listed on the Harare Memorial in the Pioneer Cemetery. Source: CWGC.

Surname	Name	Number	Rank	Status	DoD	Footnote
Kongoshora		M2083	Pte	DOAS	21/10/1918	Died of unknown cause. Source: NAZ and *Masodja*. Listed on the Harare Memorial in the Pioneer Cemetery. Source: CWGC.
Kurakura		5035	N Cst	DOAS	17/12/1918	Died of pneumonia at Zomba, Nyasaland. From BSAP. Source: NAZ.
Kuzwarera		M2242	Pte	DOAS	29/10/1918	Source: *Masodja*. Unlikely African name and no information.
Kwanda		7	N Cst	DOAS	04/10/1917	Died from dysentery at Songea, GEA (Tanzania). From BSAP. Source: NAZ.
Lita		M115	Sgt	DOAS	27/10/1917	Died of natural causes at Chipambawe (country?). Also spelt Rita. Awarded Distinguished Conduct Medal and Mentioned in Despatches. Source: NAZ. Also spelt Rita.
Lopa	Dick	M1295	Pte	DOAS	14/06/1918	Died of meningitis at Mwemba, GEA (Tanzania). Also spelt Lopa. Source: NAZ and *Masodja*.
Lupiya		M114	Pte	KIA	12/11/1916	Killed at Songea, GEA (Tanzania). Source: NAZ.
Mabujana		M55	Pte	KIA	11/11/1916	Source: NAZ and *Masodja*.
Mabune		M1845	Pte	DOAS	27/07/1918	Died of diarrhoea at Ft Johnson, Nyasaland. Source: NAZ.
Madolo	Jim	M709	Pte	DOAS	25/11/1918	Died of pneumonia at Limbe, Nyasaland. Source: NAZ and *Masodja*.
Mafela		M27	Pte	KIA	29/01/1917	Also spelt Mafelo. Source: NAZ and *Masodja*.
Magugwana		M4	Pte	KIA	23/10/1916	Also spelt Nagugwana (unlikely). Source: NAZ and *Masodja*.
Mahina		M700	Pte	DOAS	29/01/1918	Died of dysentery at Mbambaba, Nyasaland. Source: NAZ and *Masodja*.
Mahwatsine		M1584	Pte	DOAS	10/12/1918	Died of pneumonia at Ntondwe, Nyasaland. Also spelt Magwatsine (unlikely). Source: NAZ.
Maida		M759	Pte	DOAS	11/12/1918	Died of pneumonia at Ntondwe, Nyasaland. Source: NAZ and *Masodja*.
Makohliso		M388	Pte	DOAS	09/07/1918	Died of dysentery in GEA (Tanzania). Source: NAZ and *Masodja*.
Makungai		M97	Pte	DOAS	13/04/1917	Died of exhaustion at Zomba, Nyasaland. Also spelt Makumgai (unlikely). Source: NAZ and *Masodja*.
Makamba		M948	Pte	KIA	22/08/1918	Also spelt Makwamba. Source: NAZ and *Masodja*.
Malamba	Office	M2059	Pte	DOAS	09/12/1918	Died of pneumonia at Ntondwe, Nyasaland. Source: NAZ and *Masodja*.
Maluwa		4780	N Cst	DOAS	08/08/1917	Died of pneumonia at Peramiho, GEA (Tanzania). Also spelt Maluna (unlikely). From BSAP. Source: NAZ.
Mandanda		M433	Pte	DOAS	U/K	Died of unknown cause. Source: NAZ.
Mangobe		M12	Pte	DOAS	28/12/1916	Died of malaria. Also spelt Mangobi (unlikely). Source: NAZ and *Masodja*.
Mangoshi		5293	N Cst	DOAS	14/12/1918	Died of pneumonia at Ntondwe, Nyasaland. Also spelt Mangoche. From BSAP. Source: NAZ.
Mangola		M394	Pte	DOAS	24/06/1918	Died of pleurisy in East Africa. Source: NAZ.
Manja		M1984	Pte	DOAS	26/10/1918	Died of unknown cause. Source: NAZ and *Masodja*. Listed on the Harare Memorial in the Pioneer Cemetery. Source: CWGC.
Manolole		M443	Pte	KIA	23/03/1917	Died of wounds. Source: NAZ.
Mantandi		M2006	L Cpl	DOAS	23/10/1918	Source: *Masodja*. Listed on the Harare Memorial in the Pioneer Cemetery. Source: CWGC.
Manyola		M1394	Pte	DOAS	24/06/1918	Died of unknown cause. Source: NAZ.

Surname	Name	Number	Rank	Status	DoD	Footnote
Maoko		M314	Pte	DOAS	01/10/1918	Died of heart failure in Salisbury. Also spelt Maoka (unlikely). Source: NAZ and *Masodja*. Listed on the Harare Memorial in the Pioneer Cemetery. Source: CWGC.
Maretea		M1420	Pte	DOAS	03/12/1918	Died of pneumonia at Ntondwe, Nyasaland. Source: NAZ.
Masandiko		M854	Pte	DOAS	03/12/1918	Died of pneumonia at Ntondwe, Nyasaland. Source: NAZ and *Masodja*.
Masanka		M1217	Pte	DOAS	02/12/1918	Died of pneumonia at Liwonde, Nyasaland. Also spelt Wasanka. Source: NAZ.
Masoja		M2026	Pte	KIA	05/09/1918	Also spelt Masoia (unlikely). Source: NAZ and *Masodja*.
Matjudula		M381	Pte	DOAS	30/08/1917	Died of pneumonia. Also spelt Matjubundula. Source: NAZ and *Masodja*.
Matobo		M1366	Pte	DOAS	15/07/1918	Died of rheumatism at Fort Johnson, Nyasaland. Also spelt Matoba. Source: NAZ.
Matsara	Zimba	M1730	Pte	DOAS	11/12/1918	Died of pneumonia at Ntondwe, Nyasaland. Source: NAZ and *Masodja*.
Mavura		M1670	Pte	DOAS	20/05/1918	Died of inknown cause at Msangesi, GEA (Tanzania). Source: NAZ.
Mbile		M1335	A Cpl	DOAS	02/12/1918	Died of pneumonia at Limbe, Nyasaland. Source: NAZ and *Masodja*.
Mdala	Mbaluka	M1099	Pte	DOAS	15/12/1918	Died of pneumonia at Ntondwe, Nyasaland. Source: NAZ.
Mgawana		M1073	Pte	DOAS	13/08/1913	Died of dysentery at Mlanje, Nyasaland. Also spelt Mcawana (unlikely). Source: NAZ and *Masodja*.
Mkotiswa		M1361	Pte	DOAS	10/03/1918	Died of dysentery at Chinde, PEA (Mozambique). Source: NAZ.
Mrewa		M1738	Pte	DOAS	U/K	Died of unknown cause. Source: NAZ and *Masodja*.
Mrewa		M2155	Pte	DOAS	25/10/1918	Listed on the Harare Memorial in the Pioneer Cemetery. Source: CWGC.
Msindo		M991	Pte	DOAS	02/08/1917	Died of unknown cause. Source: NAZ and *Masodja*. Listed on the Harare Memorial in the Pioneer Cemetery. Source: CWGC.
Msunyana		M1330	Pte	DOAS	07/12/1918	Died of pneumonia at Ntondwe, Nyasaland. Source: NAZ.
Mtaro		M1744	Pte	DOAS	10/12/1918	Died of arthritis at Ft Johnson, Nyasaland. Source: NAZ and *Masodja*.
Mtema		M84	Pte	KIA	09/11/1916	Source: NAZ and *Masodja*.
Mtima		M2045	Pte	DOAS	U/K	Died of unknown cause. Source: NAZ.
Mtembe		4448	N Sgt	DOAS	U/K	Died of unknown cause. From BSAP. Source: NAZ.
Mubeta		M1764	Pte	DOAS	07/03/1918	Died of pneumonia at Mtengula, Nyasaland. Also spelt Mubita (unlikely). Source: NAZ and *Masodja*.
Musgrave	Gerald Harry	MR/40	Sgt	DOAS	14/12/1918	Died of pneumonia at Zomba, Nyasaland, aged 37 years. Born in London, England. He is buried in the Zomba Town Cemetery, Malawi. Ex-2RR Private (service number 660, enlisted 10 Sept 1916), seeing service in GEA. Source: CWGC, NAZ, Capell and Masodja.
Mwalema	Jim	M1901	Pte	DOAS	12/12/1918	Died of pneumonia at Ntondwe, Nyasaland. Also spelt Mulema. Also listed as 2RR (?). Source: NAZ and *Masodja*.
Mwalema		M1578	Pte	DOAS	21/12/1918	Died of pneumonia at Ntondwe, Nyasaland. Source: NAZ and *Masodja*.
Myumba		M1690	Pte	DOAS	11/12/1918	Died of pneumonia at Ntondwe, Nyasaland. Source: NAZ and *Masodja*.
Nadi			Pte	DOAS	U/K	Source: Masodja. Unlikely African name and no information

Surname	Name	Number	Rank	Status	DoD	Footnote
Nana		M1272	Pte	DOAS	10/12/1918	Died of pneumonia at Ntondwe, Nyasaland. Source: NAZ and *Masodja*.
Nandi	William	M746	Pte	DOAS	09/12/1918	Died of pneumonia at Ntondwe, Nyasaland. Also spelt Nadi (unlikely). Source: NAZ and *Masodja*.
Ndara		M1462	A Cpl	KOAS	29/05/1918	Died of a gunshot wound at Mtarika in GEA (Tanzania). Source: NAZ.
Ndarira		M61	Pte	DOAS	15/11/1917	Died of unknown cause. Source: NAZ.
Ndowa		M1936	L Cpl	DOAS	17/08/1918	Died of diarrhoea in East Africa. Source: NAZ.
Nduga		M1175	Pte	DOAS	27/12/1918	Died of dysentery at Blantyre, Nyasaland. Source: NAZ and *Masodja*.
Nduka	Charlie	M555	Pte	DOAS	02/12/1918	Died of pneumonia at Limbe, Nyasaland. Source: NAZ and Masodja.
Nduna		M1338	Pte	DOAS	U/K	Died of unknown cause. Source: NAZ.
Ndura		M1328	Pte	DOAS	04/12/1918	Died of pneumonia at Ntondwe, Nyasaland. Source: NAZ and *Masodja*.
Ngunyama		M1357	Pte	DOAS	17/12/1918	Died of pneumonia at Ntondwe, Nyasaland. Also spelt Ngunyana. Source: NAZ and *Masodja*.
Njube		M2277	Pte	DOAS	30/10/1918	Source: *Masodja*. Listed on the Harare Memorial in the Pioneer Cemetery. Source: CWGC.
Nkuhlana		4480	N Cst	DOAS	28/02/1918	Died of enteric fever at Ft Johnson, Nyasaland. From BSAP. Source: NAZ and *Masodja*.
Nkulunyelwa		M448	Pte	KIA	23/03/1917	Father of Senator Chief Kayisa Ndiweni. Also spelt Mkulunyelwa. Source: NAZ and *Masodja*.
Noma		M1261	Pte	DOAS	04/01/1919	Died of pneumonia at Zomba, Nyasaland. Source: NAZ and *Masodja*.
Ntemba		4448	N Sgt	DOAS	14/10/1918	Died of small pox in East Africa. Also spelt Ntembe. Source: NAZ and *Masodja*.
Ntubane		M353	Pte	KIA	26/08/1917	Died of wounds. Also spelt Ntubne (unlikely). Source NAZ and *Masodja*.
Nyatsi		M356	Pte	KIA	30/08/1917	Also spelt Mnyatsi (unlikely). Source: NAZ and *Masodja*.
Nyelenda	Philip	M1892	Sgt	DOAS	12/11/1918	Died of pneumonia in East Africa. Source: NAZ.
Nyukwa (see footnote)		M263	Pte	KOAS	16/01/1917	Killed by a lion. Name also found as Nyuka. Alernative DoD 12 Jan 1917. Source: NAZ and *Masodja*.
Pabanga		M427	Pte	DOAS	20/03/1917	He is said to have died of disease while a POW, after having been captured at St Moritz, GEA (Tanzania). Source: NAZ and *Masodja*.
Perange		M1080	Pte	DOAS	26/10/1917	Also spelt Paranje (unlikely). Died of unknown cause. Source: NAZ and *Masodja*. Listed on the Harare Memorial in the Pioneer Cemetery. Source: CWGC.
Piggin	Frederick Percy Loverseed	Not issued	Lt	KIA	20/12/1916	Killed at Zomesa, near Songea, GEA (Tanzania), aged 29 years. From BSAP Salisbury. (1215 attest: 07 Mar 1910). Source: NAZ and *Masodja*. Buried in the Dar es Salaam War Cemetery, Tanzania.
Ponsipansi		M88	Pte	KIA	07/11/1916	Also spelt Ponsiponsi (unlikely). Source: NAZ and Masodja.
Punganama		M154	Pte	MIA	10/02/1917	Missing believed dead. Source: NAZ and *Masodja*.
Ranhamuiss		M1502	Pte	DOAS	23/08/1918	Died of unknown cause. Source: NAZ. (This name seems very unlikely).
Rutherfoord	Arthur Henry	Not issued	Lt	KIA	23/07/1917	Killed at the Ruhudje River, near Mpepo in GEA (Tanzania). Died aged 27 years, buried in the Iringa Cemetery, Tanzania. Source: CWGC, NAZ and *Masodja*. Ex-2RR Sgt (number 497 enlisted 27 Oct 1914).
Sabati	Sabobi	M1651	Pte	DOAS	18/10/1918	Died of unknown cause in East Africa. Source: NAZ.

Surname	Name	Number	Rank	Status	DoD	Footnote
Sadi		M1830	Pte	DOAS	U/K	Died of unknown cause. Source: NAZ.
Salanda		M497	Pte	DOAS	29/10/1918	Died of influenza, Salisbury. Source: NAZ and *Masodja*. Listed on the Harare Memorial in the Pioneer Cemetery. Source: CWGC.
Salani	Sam	M827	Pte	DOAS	14/12/1918	Died of pneumonia at Ntondwe, Nyasaland. Also spelt Sakani. Source: NAZ.
Samlinda		M581	Pte	DOAS	25/05/1917	Died of unknown cause. Source: NAZ and *Masodja*. Listed on the Harare Memorial in the Pioneer Cemetery. Source: CWGC.
Shimwazi		M1982	Pte	DOAS	26/02/1918	Died of pnemonia at Mtengula, Nyasaland. Source: NAZ.
Shituma	Mtenga	M554	Pte	DOAS	05/12/1918	Died of pneumonia at Ntondwe, Nyasaland. Source: NAZ.
Sigupa	Jack	M567	Pte	DOAS	04/12/1918	Died of pneumonia at Ntondwe, Nyasaland. Source: NAZ and Masodja.
Sikotu		M2	Pte	KIA	23/10/1916	Died of wounds. Source: NAZ and Masodja.
Sikuka		M1491	Pte	DOAS	09/12/1918	Died of pneumonia at Ntondwe, Nyasaland. Also spelt Sikuku. Source: NAZ.
Simila	Nleja	M1858	Pte	DOAS	02/11/1918	Died of dysentery and pneumonia at Namweri. Source: NAZ.
Simone		M241	Pte	KIA	29/01/1917	Also spelt Simono. Source: NAZ and *Masodja*
Simpson	Hector Joseph	Not issued	Lt	KIA	29/01/1917	Killed at Kitanda in East Africa. From BSAP Lomagundi, Hartley and Melsetter (No. 417 attest: 29 Nov 1902). Source: NAZ and *Masodja*. Died aged 29 years. Buried in the Iringa Cemetery, Tanzania. Source: CWGC.
Sitampa		M2077	Pte	DOAS	22/12/1917	Died of unknown cause. Also spelt Sitamba. Source: NAZ and *Masodja*. Listed on the Harare Memorial in the Pioneer Cemetery. Source: CWGC.
Sitifano		M1726	Pte	DOAS	12/05/1918	Died of pnemonia at Mwemba in GEA (Tanzania). Source: NAZ.
Smart	William		Pte	MIA	24/04/1918	Missing presumed killed. Ex 2RR. Source: NAZ.
Tamalin		M804	Pte	DOAS	15/12/1918	Died of pneumonia at Ntondwe, Nyasaland. Source: NAZ.
Tantwe		M198	Pte	KIA	04/09/1917	Died of wounds. Source: NAZ.
Tawulo		M1584	Pte	DOAS	05/06/1916	Died of unknown cause. Source: NAZ and *Masodja*. Listed on the Harare Memorial in the Pioneer Cemetery. Source: CWGC.
Tenkenyika		M1725	Pte	DOAS	13/12/1918	Died at Blantyre, Nyasaland. Source: NAZ.
Terry	Charles Warwick		CQMS	DOAS	05/11/1918	Died of influenza. Source: NAZ.
Tirana	Moses	M1660	Pte	DOAS	31/05/1918	Died of pulmonary tuberculosis in GEA (Tanzania). Source: NAZ and *Masodja*.
Tonati		M643	Pte	DOAS	04/01/1919	Died of pneumonia at Zomba, Nyasaland. Source: NAZ.
Umsapakesa		31	N Sgt	DOAS	19/10/1918	Died of unknown causes. From BSAP. Source: NAZ. Listed as BSAP on the Harare Memorial in the Pioneer Cemetery. Source: CWGC.
Wasili		M477	Pte	KIA	07/11/1916	DoD also listed as 2 November. Source: NAZ.
Williams	John Howard	Not issued	Lt	KIA	19/08/1917	Died from wounds received at Mpepo, GEA (Tanzania). Died aged 25 years, buried in the Iringa Cemetery, Tanzania. He was born in Bechuanaland. Ex-2RR Private (service number 796, enlisted 5 Dec 1914). Source: NAZ, Capell and Masodja.

Surname	Name	Number	Rank	Status	DoD	Footnote
Winter	Alfred Paul Delaffe	1396	Sgt	DOAS	20/12/1918	Died of pneumonia at Zomba, Nyasaland, aged 29 years. He is buried in the Zomba Town Cemetery, Malawi, where he is listed as RNR. From BSAP. Source: CWGC, NAZ and Masodja.
Yago	Jack	M492	Pte	DOAS	12/12/1918	Died of pneumonia at Ntondwe, Nyasaland. Source: NAZ and *Masodja*.
Yesaya		M1840	Pte	DOAS	10/12/1918	Died of pneumonia at Ntondwe, Nyasaland. Source: NAZ.
Zanda		M2091	Pte	DOAS	28/10/1918	Source: *Masodja*. Listed on the Harare Memorial in the Pioneer Cemetery. Source: CWGC.
Zauwa		M177	Pte	DOAS	16/06/1918	Died of diarrhoea. Source: NAZ.
Zilde		4798	Sgt	KIA	10/11/1916	Source: NAZ. (Strongly believe this is the same as the one immediately below. Almost certain the surname is Zilde, and in the absence of a typewriter, easy mistake. Service numbers very close.)
Ziloli		4778	Cpl	KIA	10/11/1916	Killed at Songea, GEA (Tanzania). From the BSAP. Source: NAZ.
Zinchetera		M154	Pte	KIA	29/01/1917	Also spelt Zinchetere. Source: NAZ and *Masodja*.
Zinzi		M428	Pte	KIA	27/07/1917	Also spelt Zinsi (unlikely). Source: NAZ and *Masodja*.
Ziyayi		M2286	Pte	DOAS	23/10/1918	Source: *Masodja*. Listed on the Harare Memorial in the Pioneer Cemetery. Source: CWGC.
Zunze	Roman	M526	Pte	DOAS	09/12/1918	Died of pneumonia at Ntondwe, Nyasaland. Also spelt Zunzi (unlikley) Source: NAZ.
Zuwa		M2034	L Cpl	DOAS	22/10/1918	Died of unknown cause. Source: *Masodja*. Listed on the Harare Memorial in the Pioneer Cemetery. Source: CWGC.

Chapter 4

Roll of Honour: 1RAR WWII and Malaya

Surname	Name	Number	Rank	Status	DoD	Footnote
Abero		RHO/1105	Pte	KIA	26/04/1945	Died in the battle of Taungup, the Arakan, Burma. No known grave. Listed on the Rangoon War Memorial in the Taukkyan Cemetery, Myanmar (Burma). Source: CWGC and *Masodja*.
Chamba		2823	Pte	DOAS	27/05/1946	Buried in the War Graves Plot, Pioneer Cemetery, Harare. Source: CWGC and *Masodja*.
Chigodo	D	RHO/1786	Pte	DOAS	20/11/1944	Died while serving in Ceylon. Grave not found. Listed on the Colombo (Liveramentu) War Memorial Tablets in Colombo, Sri Lanka. Source: CWGC and *Masodja*.
Chigwadi		2213	Pte	DOAS	22/04/1944	Buried in the War Graves Plot, Pioneer Cemetery, Harare. Source: CWGC and *Masodja*.
Chikami		1664	Pte	DOAS	29/10/1942	Buried in the War Graves Plot, Pioneer Cemetery, Harare. Source: CWGC and *Masodja*.
Chikange		RHO/691	L Cpl	KIA	26/04/1945	Died in the battle of Taungup, the Arakan, Burma. No known grave. Listed on the Rangoon War Memorial in the Taukkyan Cemetery, Myanmar (Burma). Source: CWGC and *Masodja*.
Chiwoni		RHO/1883	Pte	KIA	05/05/1945	Died in Burma. No known grave. Listed on the Rangoon War Memorial in the Taukkyan Cemetery, Myanmar (Burma). Source: CWGC and *Masodja*.
Coulthard	McDonald	X2318	Sgt	DOAS	30/04/1941	Buried in the War Graves Plot, Pioneer Cemetery, Harare. Source: CWGC and *Masodja*.
Crispin		RHO/114	L Cpl	KIA	24/04/1945	Died in Burma. No known grave. Listed on the Rangoon War Memorial in the Taukkyan Cemetery, Myanmar (Burma). Source: CWGC and *Masodja*.
Danda		317	Pte	DOAS	23/12/1941	Buried in the War Graves Plot, Pioneer Cemetery, Harare. Source: CWGC and *Masodja*.
Daniel	George Fleck	X5478	Sgt	DOAS	17/11/1945	Buried in the War Graves Plot, Pioneer Cemetery, Harare. Source: CWGC and *Masodja*. Service number in *Masodja* listed as GR2748.
Dick		RHO/1158	Pte	KIA	26/04/1945	Died in the battle of Taungup, the Arakan, Burma. No known grave. Listed on the Rangoon War Memorial in the Taukkyan Cemetery, Myanmar (Burma). Source: CWGC and *Masodja*.
Dimingu	Tom	RHO/208	Pte	KIA	04/05/1945	Died in Burma. No known grave. Listed on the Rangoon War Memorial in the Taukkyan Cemetery, Myanmar (Burma). Source: CWGC and *Masodja*.
Donald		RHO/1934	Pte	KIA	05/05/1945	Buried in the Maynamati War Cemetery, Bangladesh. Source: CWGC and *Masodja*.
Egeler	Thomas Humphrey	X5482	Sgt	DOAS	29/02/1944	Buried in the War Graves Plot, Pioneer Cemetery, Harare. Source: CWGC and *Masodja*.
Elias		2179	Pte	DOAS	08/07/1946	Buried in the War Graves Plot, Pioneer Cemetery, Harare. Source: CWGC and *Masodja*.
Embruku		RHO/1889	Pte	KIA	26/04/1945	Died in the battle of Taungup, the Arakan, Burma. No known grave. Listed on the Rangoon War Memorial in the Taukkyan Cemetery, Myanmar (Burma). Source: CWGC and *Masodja*.
Fanyana		2241	Pte	DOAS	22/02/1944	Buried in the War Graves Plot, Pioneer Cemetery, Harare. Source: CWGC.
Fred		RHO/1570	Pte	KIA	19/10/1945	Buried in the Chittagong War Cemetery, Bangladesh. Sourec: CWGC and *Masodja*.
Hlome		2242	Pte	DOAS	22/02/1944	Buried in the War Graves Plot, Pioneer Cemetery, Harare. Source: CWGC and *Masodja*.
Imonda		RHO/4096	Pte	KIA	26/04/1945	Died in the battle of Taungup, the Arakan, Burma. No known grave. Listed on the Rangoon War Memorial in the Taukkyan Cemetery, Myanmar (Burma). Source: CWGC and *Masodja*.

Surname	Name	Number	Rank	Status	DoD	Footnote
Jack		RHO/2207	Pte	KIA	14/01/1945	Died in Burma. No known grave. Listed on the Rangoon War Memorial in the Taukkyan Cemetery, Myanmar (Burma). Source: CWGC and *Masodja*.
Jaisi		1736	Pte	DOAS	05/05/1946	Listed on the Bulawayo African War Memorial in the Lady Stanley Avenue Cemetery, Bulawayo. Grave unknown. Source: CWGC.
James		2795	Pte	DOAS	20/09/1945	Buried in the War Graves Plot, Pioneer Cemetery, Harare. Source: CWGC and *Masodja*.
Joel		RHO/1127	Sgt	DOAS	14/02/1946	Died on active service in India. Grave not found. Listed on the Kirkee 1939-45 War Memorial in the Kirkee Cemetery in Poona, near Bombay, India. Source: CWGC.
Johane		RHO/2122	Pte	DOAS	13/07/1946	Died in Burma. No known grave. Listed on the Rangoon War Memorial in the Taukkyan Cemetery, Myanmar (Burma). Source: CWGC.
Joseph		4116	Pte	DOAS	26/07/1944	Buried in the Lady Stanley Avenue Cemetery, Bulawayo. Source: CWGC and *Masodja*.
Joseni		4115	Pte	KIA	03/04/1945	Died in Burma. No known grave. Listed on the Rangoon War Memorial in the Taukkyan Cemetery, Myanmar (Burma). Source: CWGC and Masodja. Listed in *Masodja* as Joseph.
Kanamanyanga		2737	Pte	KIA	09/11/1944	Listed on the Bulawayo African War Memorial in the Lady Stanley Avenue Cemetery, Bulawayo. Grave unknown. Source: CWGC and *Masodja*.
Kaswaurere		1258	Pte	DOAS	28/01/1943	Buried in the War Graves Plot, Pioneer Cemetery, Harare. Source: CWGC.
Kenny	Gordon H.M.	X3137	Sgt	DOAS	17/07/1941	Died aged 24 years. Buried in the War Graves Plot, Pioneer Cemetery, Harare. Source: CWGC.
Kodzayi		1331	Pte	DOAS	20/05/1946	Buried in the War Graves Plot, Pioneer Cemetery, Harare. Source: CWGC.
Lazalosi		31	L Cpl	KIA	26/04/1945	Died in the battle of Taungup, the Arakan, Burma. No known grave. Listed on the Rangoon War Memorial in the Taukkyan Cemetery, Myanmar (Burma). Source: CWGC and *Masodja*.
Lichanda		506	WOI	DOAS	17/10/1942	Buried in the War Graves Plot, Pioneer Cemetery, Harare. Source: CWGC.
Loya	Gwelo	1460	Pte	KIA	13/04/1945	Died in Burma. No known grave. Listed on the Rangoon War Memorial in the Taukkyan Cemetery, Myanmar (Burma). Source: CWGC and *Masodja*.
Malenga	Peter	1968	Pte	KIA	04/04/1944	Buried in the Moshi Military Cemetery in Moshi, Tanzania. Source: CWGC and *Masodja*.
Mambo		RHO/4248	Pte	KIA	05/05/1945	Died in Burma. No known grave. Listed on the Rangoon War Memorial in the Taukkyan Cemetery, Myanmar (Burma). Source: CWGC and *Masodja*.
Mambwe		RHO/1779	Pte	KIA	17/04/1945	Died in Burma. No known grave. Listed on the Rangoon War Memorial in the Taukkyan Cemetery, Myanmar (Burma). Source: CWGC and *Masodja*.
Managalazi		624	Pte	DOAS	06/01/1941	Buried in the War Graves Plot, Pioneer Cemetery, Harare. Source: CWGC.
Mangoni		RHO/1373	Pte	KIA	05/05/1945	Died in Burma. No known grave. Listed on the Rangoon War Memorial in the Taukkyan Cemetery, Myanmar (Burma). Source: CWGC and *Masodja*.
Mapesa		2278	Pte	DOAS	18/11/1945	Buried in the War Graves Plot, Pioneer Cemetery, Harare. Source: CWGC and *Masodja*. Spelt Maoera in *Masodja* (unlikely).
Mapurisa		1810	Pte	KIA	21/08/1943	Listed on the Bulawayo African War Memorial in the Lady Stanley Avenue Cemetery, Bulawayo. Grave unknown. Source: CWGC and *Masodja*.
Matake		4347	Pte	DOAS	30/03/1946	Buried in the Lady Stanley Avenue Cemetery, Bulawayo. Source: CWGC.
Mbayiwa		243	Pte	DOAS	08/09/1942	Buried in the War Graves Plot, Pioneer Cemetery, Harare. Source: CWGC and *Masodja*.

Surname	Name	Number	Rank	Status	DoD	Footnote
Mundiya		RHO/4152	Pte	KIA	13/04/1945	Died in Burma. No known grave. Listed on the Rangoon War Memorial in the Taukkyan Cemetery, Myanmar (Burma). Source: CWGC and *Masodja*.
Munyuki	J	RHO/4245	Pte	KIA	10/04/1945	Died in Burma. No known grave. Listed on the Rangoon War Memorial in the Taukkyan Cemetery, Myanmar (Burma). Source: CWGC and *Masodja*.
Musekiwa		RHO/1268	Pte	DOAS	31/01/1946	Buried in the Rangoon War Cemetery, Myanmar (Burma). Source: CWGC.
Muyeya		1853	L Cpl	KIA	09/02/1945	Listed on the Lusaka 1939-45 War Memorial in the Burma Barracks, Lusaka, Zambia. Source: CWGC and *Masodja*.
Muzanzi		1591	Pte	KIA	28/10/1942	Listed on the Bulawayo African War Memorial in the Lady Stanley Avenue Cemetery, Bulawayo. Grave unknown. Source: CWGC and *Masodja*. Spelt Muzadzi by CWGC.
Ndoro		RHO/800	Pte	KIA	26/04/1945	Died in the battle of Taungup, the Arakan, Burma. No known grave. Listed on the Rangoon War Memorial in the Taukkyan Cemetery, Myanmar (Burma). Source: CWGC and *Masodja*. Spelt Ndodo by CWGC.
Neapiyara		RHO/642	Pte	KIA	29/04/1945	Died in Burma. No known grave. Listed on the Rangoon War Memorial in the Taukkyan Cemetery, Myanmar (Burma). Source: CWGC and *Masodja*.
Ngezi		3596	Pte	DOAS	25/06/1945	Buried in the War Graves Plot, Pioneer Cemetery, Harare. Source: CWGC.
Nyagumbo		RHO/2329	Pte	KIA	27/03/1945	Died in Burma. No known grave. Listed on the Rangoon War Memorial in the Taukkyan Cemetery, Myanmar (Burma). Source: CWGC.
Pikita	Sam	RHO/1211	Pte	KIA	27/04/1945	Died in the battle of Taungup, the Arakan, Burma. No known grave. Listed on the Rangoon War Memorial in the Taukkyan Cemetery, Myanmar (Burma). Source: CWGC and *Masodja*.
Piyo		316	Pte	KIA	22/12/1944	Listed on the Lusaka 1939-45 War Memorial in the Burma Barracks, Lusaka, Zambia. Source: CWGC and *Masodja*.
Ronald		RHO/2315	Pte	KIA	26/04/1945	Died in the battle of Taungup, the Arakan, Burma. No known grave. Listed on the Rangoon War Memorial in the Taukkyan Cemetery, Myanmar (Burma). Source: CWGC and *Masodja*.
Ruzvidzo		RHO/592	Pte	KIA	26/04/1945	Died in the battle of Taungup, the Arakan, Burma. No known grave. Listed on the Rangoon War Memorial in the Taukkyan Cemetery, Myanmar (Burma). Source: CWGC and *Masodja*.
Semu		RHO/2363	Pte	DOAS	12/08/1945	Buried in the Rangoon War Cemetery, Myanmar (Burma). Source: CWGC and *Masodja*.
Shelome		RHO/4133	Pte	KIA	24/04/1945	Died in Burma. No known grave. Listed on the Rangoon War Memorial in the Taukkyan Cemetery, Myanmar (Burma). Source: CWGC and *Masodja*.
Sikonzi		RHO/4238	Pte	KIA	17/04/1945	Died in Burma. No known grave. Listed on the Rangoon War Memorial in the Taukkyan Cemetery, Myanmar (Burma). Source: CWGC.
Silimbwana		880	Pte	KIA	26/04/1945	Died in the battle of Taungup, the Arakan, Burma. No known grave. Listed on the Rangoon War Memorial in the Taukkyan Cemetery, Myanmar (Burma). Source: CWGC and Masodja. Spelt Solombwana in *Masodja*.
Simasiku		RHO/4193	Pte	DOAS	12/06/1945	Buried in the Maynamati Military Cemetery, Bangladesh. Source: CWGC and *Masodja*.
Simon		1152	Pte	KIA	26/04/1945	Died in the battle of Taungup, the Arakan, Burma. No known grave. Listed on the Rangoon War Memorial in the Taukkyan Cemetery, Myanmar (Burma). Source: CWGC and *Masodja*.
Soda	Finasi	RHO/1306	Pte	KIA	09/11/1945	Buried in the Maynamati Military Cemetery, Bangladesh. Source: CWGC and *Masodja*.
Tagula		4957	Pte	DOAS	31/10/1946	Buried in the Lady Stanley Avenue Cemetery, Bulawayo. Source: CWGC.
Tagwira		RHO/907	Pte	KIA	05/05/1945	Died in Burma. No known grave. Listed on the Rangoon War Memorial in the Taukkyan Cemetery, Myanmar (Burma). Source: CWGC and *Masodja*. Spelt Kagwira by CWGC.
Takawira		RHO/1060	Pte	KIA	13/04/1945	Died in Burma. No known grave. Listed on the Rangoon War Memorial in the Taukkyan Cemetery, Myanmar (Burma). Source: CWGC and *Masodja*.

Surname	Name	Number	Rank	Status	DoD	Footnote
Taliya		RHO/36	Cpl	KIA	22/01/1945	Died in Burma. No known grave. Listed on the Rangoon War Memorial in the Taukkyan Cemetery, Myanmar (Burma). Source: CWGC and *Masodja*.
Tambudzai		444	Pte	KIA	21/12/1945	Died in Burma. No known grave. Listed on the Rangoon War Memorial in the Taukkyan Cemetery, Myanmar (Burma). Source: CWGC and *Masodja*.
Tawaziwa		RHO/1689	Pte	KIA	26/04/1945	Died in the battle of Taungup, the Arakan, Burma. No known grave. Listed on the Rangoon War Memorial in the Taukkyan Cemetery, Myanmar (Burma). Source: CWGC and *Masodja*.
Tawona		RHO/1976	Pte	DOAS	03/04/1946	Buried in the Nairobi War Cemetery, Kenya. Source: CWGC.
Thomas		2596	Pte	DOAS	13/05/1945	Buried in the War Graves Plot, Pioneer Cemetery, Harare. Source: CWGC.
Timotiya		RHO/1816	Pte	KIA	26/04/1945	Died in the battle of Taungup, the Arakan, Burma. No known grave. Listed on the Rangoon War Memorial in the Taukkyan Cemetery, Myanmar (Burma). Source: CWGC and *Masodja*.
Tirivanhu		RHO/2146	Pte	KIA	26/04/1945	Died in the battle of Taungup, the Arakan, Burma. No known grave. Listed on the Rangoon War Memorial in the Taukkyan Cemetery, Myanmar (Burma). Source: CWGC and *Masodja*. Spelt Timitiya in *Masodja*.
Tongwe		3099	Pte	DOAS	15/04/1945	Buried in the War Graves Plot, Pioneer Cemetery, Harare. Source: CWGC.
Wachekwa		RHO/1920	Pte	DOAS	24/10/1944	Died while serving in Ceylon. Grave not found. Listed on the Colombo (Liveramentu) War Memorial Tablets in Colombo, Sri Lanka. Source: CWGC and *Masodja*.
Watson	Benjamin Robert	SR/2748	Sgt	DOAS	10/04/1944	Buried in the War Graves Plot, Pioneer Cemetery, Harare. Source: CWGC.
Wilson		1397	Cpl	DOAS	11/10/1943	Buried in the War Graves Plot, Pioneer Cemetery, Harare. Source: CWGC.
Yotam		1944	Cpl	DOAS	08/07/1945	Buried in the War Graves Plot, Pioneer Cemetery, Harare. Source: CWGC.
Zawake		663	Pte	DOAS	04/06/1945	Buried in the War Graves Plot, Pioneer Cemetery, Harare. Source: CWGC and *Masodja*. Spelt Suwake in *Masodja*.
Zilole		499	Sgt	DOAS	04/01/1944	Listed on the Lubudi War Memorial in the Democratic Republic of the Congo. There are only eight names of WWII Commonwealth casualties inscribed on the memorial. Source: CWGC and *Masodja*.
Zimurawa		RHO/993	Pte	DOAS	25/03/1946	Buried in the Rangoon War Cemetery, Myanmar (Burma). Source: CWGC.
Zvidzayi		RHO/1379	Cpl	KIA	05/05/1945	Died in Burma. No known grave. Listed on the Rangoon War Memorial in the Taukkyan Cemetery, Myanmar (Burma). Source: CWGC and *Masodja*. Spelt Zwizayi by CWGC.

Roll of Honour: 1RAR Malaya and Canal Zone

Billy		3430	Pte	KOAS	02/10/1952	Died in the Suez Canal Zone Crisis. Buried in the Moascar War Cemetery, Egypt.
Jonah		4766	Pte	KOAS	24/09/1957	Died in the Malaya Emergency. Buried in the Kranji Military Cemetery, Singapore.
Joseph		1807	Pte	KOAS	30/05/1957	Died in the Malaya Emergency. Buried in the Kranji Military Cemetery, Singapore.
Mjikijelwa		9565	Pte	KOAS	01/02/1957	Died in the Malaya Emergency. Buried in the Kranji Military Cemetery, Singapore.
Tayengwa		187	Cpl	KOAS	31/12/1957	Died in the Malaya Emergency. Buried in the Kranji Military Cemetery, Singapore.
Tongogara		4762	L Cpl	KOAS	30/05/1957	Died in the Malaya Emergency. Buried in the Kranji Military Cemetery, Singapore.
Wonyana		4628	Pte	KOAS	19/07/1956	Died in the Malaya Emergency. Buried in the Kranji Military Cemetery, Singapore.

Chapter 5

Roll of Honour: 1RAR Bush War

Surname	Name	Number	Award	Rank	Unit	Status	DoD	Footnotes
Ainslie	Michael John Forbes "Mike"	780644		Maj	A Coy, 1st Bn	KIA	27/03/1976	Killed in a helicopter hit by ground fire whilst commanding a Fire Force action, Ngarwe TTL, Mtoko, *Op Hurricane*. Died aged 28. Cremated in Bulawayo. Source: Death Notice.
Anasi	Ignasio Mugani	R43702		Pte	1st Bn	KIA	22/01/1970	Killed by a gunshot wound in a contact on *Op Teak* south of the Victoria Falls. Died aged 29. Buried in Bikita District. Source: Death Notice. This would almost certainly not have been his surname, but his first name - a not uncommon habit back then of clerical "errors." Sadly, we may never know his surname, which is so important in tracing our black soldiers' tribal background.
Bennett	Thomas Hart	780755		Officer	1st Bn	KOAS	20/11/1970	Died in a vehicle accident on the Salisbury/Bulawayo road. Born in South Africa, he was 23 years old and was cremated at West Park, Bulawayo. Source: Death Notice.
Bickle	Albany Charles "Charlie"	V3678		2LT	1st Bn	KOAS	08/12/1977	Died in a vehicle accident on the Bulawayo-Vic Falls road, *Op Tangent*. He had popped in to see his father on their farm in Nyamandhlovu and was hurrying back to join the convoy. Source: Neill Jackson (ex-Capt RLI). A Plumtree School old boy
Boyina	Magara	644660		Cpl	1st Bn	KOAS	08/04/1977	Died in a vehicle accident. Source: Craig Fourie.
Celestino - not his surname	Celestino B.	645270		Pte	1st Bn	KIA	31/08/1975	Killed by a gunshot wound in a contact, Umfurudzi Wild Life Area, Shamva, *Op Hurricane*. Died aged 27. Source: Death Notice.
Chaka	Emmanuel	646317		Pte	1st Bn	KIA	13/06/1976	Died from gunshot wounds in a contact, *Op Hurricane*. Died aged 19. Source: Death Notice.
Chapange	Phinias	R43804		Pte	Regt Band, HQ Coy, 1st Bn	KOAS	19/05/1972	Drowned in the Fuller Forest, Matetsi area, west of Wankie, *Op Tangent*. He was 32 years old and is buried in Gutu. Source: Death Notice. Members of the band were deployed on active service, and whilst the RL they were travelling in crossed a dam wall, the vehicle fell into the water. The weight of their webbing with ammo, grenades, water, etc., pulled them under. Altogether 12 of them lost their lives in this tragic accident: P Chapange, S Dudzirayi, T Manduna, J Mangandura, K Muchato, B Murambiwa, T Ndaza, G Ngorovani, M Nyikadzino, C Ranganayi, E Takawira and M Wunganayi.
Chausina	Fanuel Nharo	R44526		Pte	C Coy, 1st Bn	KOAS	05/04/1972	Died from drowning in Kariba whilst on border control in the Deka area, northern Matabeleland. They had been picked up at the end of a patrol by a small boat with a powerful outboard motor, but upon sudden deceleration, the following wave swamped the boat. Source: Mick McKenna. He was 23 years old. Source: Death Notice. A Gwataringa and W Madziyanyika also drowned in this incident.
Chikeya	Stanley	646358		Pte	C Coy, 1st Bn	DOAS	26/02/1978	
Chikudza	Erisha	R40349		Cpl	14 Pl, E Coy, 1st Bn	KIA	18/03/1968	Killed by a gunshot wound in a contact, Urungwe, *Op Cauldron*, aged 30 years and is buried in Buhera district. Source: Death Notice.
Chimbidzukayi	Rashikayi	643492		Cpl	C Coy, 1st Bn	DOAS	03/03/1978	
Chinyani	Shadreck Misheck	R44156		Cpl	1st Bn	KIA	05/07/1973	Died from a gunshot wound in a contact, *Op Hurricane*, at the age of 27. Buried in Bulawayo. Source: Death Notice.

Surname	Name	Number	Award	Rank	Unit	Status	DoD	Footnotes
Chisora	Simon	661442		Pte	1st Bn	DOAS	12/06/1979	
Chowa	John	R43210		L Cpl	1st Bn	KOAS	21/03/1974	Died in Mpilo Hospital, Bulawayo, of multiple injuries. Died aged 33. Buried in Inyanga. Source: Death Notice.
Chuonda	Michael	644632		Pte	1st Bn	DOAS	28/05/1976	Died in a vehicle accident on the main Salisbury/Bulawayo road. He was 25 years old and is buried in Gwelo Cemetery. He was based at the School of Infantry in Gwelo. Source: Death Notice.
Davison - not his surname	Hunyena	R44904		Pte	1st Bn	KIA	08/04/1973	Died from a gunshot wound, Mazarabani TTL, Centenary, *Op Hurricane*. Died aged 19. Source: Death Notice. This would almost certainly not have been his surname, but his first name - a not uncommon habit back then of clerical "errors." Sadly, we may never know his surname, which is so important in tracing our black soldiers' tribal background.
Dennis - not his surname	Dennis - See F/note	R44158		Pte	1st Bn	KOAS	03/07/1967	This would almost certainly not have been his surname, but his first name - a not uncommon habit back then of clerical "errors." Sadly, we may never know his surname, which is so important in tracing our black soldiers' tribal background.
Dudzirayi	Silvanos Mashona	R41949		L Cpl	Regt Band, HQ Coy, 1st Bn	KOAS	19/05/1972	Drowned in the Fuller Forest, Matetsi area, west of Wankie. He was 31 years old and is buried in Bikita. Source: Death Notice. Members of the band were deployed on active service, and whilst the RL they were travelling in crossed a dam wall, the vehicle fell into the water. The weight of their webbing with ammo, grenades, water, etc., pulled them under. Altogether 12 of them lost their lives in this tragic accident: P Chapange, S Dudzirayi, T Manduna, J Mangandura, K Muchato, B Murambiwa, T Ndaza, G Ngorovani, M Nyikadzino, C Ranganayi, E Takawira and M Wunganayi.
Dzingirayi	Mukoni	646372		Pte	1st Bn	KIA	13/05/1976	Died from a gunshot wound, in a contact, in Mtoko, *Op Hurricane*. Died aged 21. Source: Death Notice.
Fisher	Jeremy Lionel	781005		Lt	A Coy, 1st Bn	DOAS	28/09/1977	A Plumtree School old boy.
Gandanga	Shandare	648478		Pte	D Coy, 1st Bn	KOAS	11/10/1978	Killed when falling from a helicopter, Mangwende TTL, *Op Hurricane*. Numerous others have commented that it is very difficult to fall out of a helicopter. It is suggested that Gandanga jumped, not realizing how far off the ground he actually was. Buried in Lady Stanley Cemetery, Bulawayo. Source: Richard Perry.
George	See F/note	R44757		Pte	1st Bn	KOAS	20/03/1973	Killed by an accidental gunshot, Sipolilo, *Op Hurricane*. He was 19 years old. Source: Death Notice. Surname not officially recorded.
Gumbo	Owen	644835		Sgt	1st Bn	KOAS	03/04/1978	Buried in Lady Stanley Cemetery, Bulawayo. Source: Richard Perry.
Gwafa	Jacob	645297		L Cpl	1st Bn	KOAS	19/04/1978	Died as a result of accidental drowning. Buried in Lady Stanley Cemetery, Bulawayo. Source: Richard Perry.
Gwatiringa	Adam Hugo	R44489		L Cpl	C Coy, 1st Bn	KOAS	05/04/1972	Died from drowning in Kariba whilst on border control in the Deka area, northern Matabeleland. They had been picked up at the end of a patrol by a small boat with a powerful outboard motor, but upon sudden deceleration, the following wave swamped the boat. Source: Mick McKenna. He was 21 years old. Source: Death Notice. F Chausina and W Madziyanyika also drowned in the same incident.
Gwenezi	Silindile	662754		Pte	1st Bn	DOAS	14/05/1979	

Surname	Name	Number	Award	Rank	Unit	Status	DoD	Footnotes
Hamandishe	John Zindoga	644775		Sgt	1st Bn	DOAS	31/03/1979	
Hardy	James William "Jim"	781083	MFC (Ops) - 11.11.78	Capt	Spt Coy 1st Bn	KIA	14/11/1978	Killed in the Mtoko area. *Op Hurricane*.
Henry - not his surname	Rodney	R43081		Cpl	1st Bn	KOAS	23/09/1974	Died in Salisbury Central Hospital from severe head injuries sustained in a vehicle accident, at the age of 36. Source: Death Notice. This would almost certainly not have been his surname, but his first name - a not uncommon habit back then of clerical "errors." Sadly, we may never know his surname, which is so important in tracing our black soldiers' tribal background.
Humanikwa	Murove	646914		Pte	1st Bn	KOAS	10/03/1977	Killed in a shooting or vehicle accident.
John - not his surname	John	645313		Pte	1st Bn	KIA	07/12/1974	Killed by a gunshot wound, Karoi, *Op Hurricane*. Died aged 21. Buried in Bulawayo. Source: Death Notice. This would almost certainly not have been his surname, but his first name - a not uncommon habit back then of clerical "errors." Sadly, we may never know his surname, which is so important in tracing our black soldiers' tribal background.
Jongwe	Shati	643975		Cpl	1st Bn	DOAS	29/05/1977	
Kambante	Korani	R43593		Pte	1st Bn	KIA	13/08/1967	Killed by a gunshot wound in a contact, near Inyantue, northern Matabeleland, JOC Wankie, *Op Nickel*. Cpl Mukombo died in the same contact.
Kangayi		644157		L Cpl	1st Bn	KIA	07/12/1974	Killed by a gunshot wound, Karoi, *Op Hurricane*. Died aged 29. Buried in Bulawayo. Source: Death Notice.
Kembo	See F/note	R43741		Cpl	1st Bn	KIA	03/08/1973	Died from a gunshot wound, Mukumbura, Mt Darwin, *Op Hurricane*. Died aged 31. Source: Death Notice. Binda's Masodja gives date as 3 March 1974, however date is correct as given on the Death Notice. Surname not officially recorded.
Kufakowenyu	Wereki Charles Mafuse	645951		Pte	1st Bn	KIA	09/08/1977	Killed in an ambush. Source: Craig Fourie.
Langton - not his surname		R44535		Pte	1st Bn	KOAS	03/03/1974	Died from severe head injuries in Mpilo Hospital, Bulawayo. He was 25 years old and is buried in Kadoma. Source: Death Notice. This would almost certainly not have been his surname, but his first name - a not uncommon habit back then of clerical "errors. Sadly, we may never know his surname, which is so important in tracing our black soldiers' tribal background.
Madzika		643553		Cpl	1st Bn	DOAS	08/09/1975	Died at Llewellin Barracks, Bulawayo, of liver failure. He was 30 years old and is buried in Gutu. Source: Death Notice.
Madziyanyika	William Jephta	R44710		Pte	C Coy, 1st Bn	KOAS	05/04/1972	Died from drowning in Kariba whilst on border control in the Deka area, northern Matabeleland. They had been picked up at the end of a patrol by a small boat with a powerful outboard motor, but upon sudden deceleration, the following wave swamped the boat. Source: Mick McKenna. His body was not found. He was 22 years old. Source: Death Notice. A Gwataringa and F Chausina also drowned in this incident.
Magara	Boyina			Cpl	1st Bn	KOAS	12/04/1977	Died in a vehicle accident. Source: Craig Fourie.
Makumbe	Alfonse	645716		L Cpl	1st Bn	KOAS	01/06/1976	Died from head injuries received in a vehicle accident in Gwelo, at the age of 19. Source: Death Notice.

Surname	Name	Number	Award	Rank	Unit	Status	DoD	Footnotes
Makuwa	James	644759	BCR (Post) - 25.03.77. See F/note	Act Cpl	A Coy, 1st Bn	KIA	09/05/1976	Killed in an ambush on his vehicle, when a 50mm mortar exploded next to him, resulting in massive haemorrhaging, Uzumba, Mrewa, *Op Hurricane*. Died aged 26. Source: Death Notice. His BCR citation states that his success in a fire force action in April 1976 was attributed to his initiative, personal courage and leadership qualities. Prior to his death he had been put forward for promotion. Source: *Masodja*.
Mambume	Andreas (Davison?)	644901		Act L Cpl	1st Bn	KIA	08/04/1973	Died from gunshot wounds.
Manaso	Jere	R44821		Pte	D Coy, 1st Bn	KIA	24/06/1973	Died from a gunshot wound, Dande TTL, Sipolilo, *Op Hurricane*. Died aged 30. Source: Death Notice.
Mandivengereyi	George	R44419		Pte	1st Bn	KOAS	06/02/1973	Died from a gunshot wound, Dande TTL, Sipolilo, *Op Hurricane*. Died aged 23. Source: Death Notice.
Manduna	Thomas	R43864		Pte	Regt Band, HQ Coy, 1st Bn	KOAS	19/05/1972	Drowned in the Fuller Forest, Matetsi area, west of Wankie. He was 26 years old and is buried in Nuanetsi. Source: Death Notice. Members of the band were deployed on active service, and whilst the RL they were travelling in crossed a dam wall, the vehicle fell into the water. The weight of their webbing with ammo, grenades, water, etc., pulled them under. Altogether 12 of them lost their lives in this tragic accident: P Chapange, S Dudzirayi, T Manduna, J Mangandura, K Muchato, B Murambiwa, T Ndaza, G Ngorovani, M Nyikadzino, C Ranganayi, E Takawira and M Wunganayi.
Mangandura	Josephat	R43761		Pte	Regt Band, HQ Coy, 1st Bn	KOAS	19/05/1972	Drowned in the Fuller Forest, Matetsi area, west of Wankie. He was 29 years old and is buried in Gutu. Source: Death Notice. Members of the band were deployed on active service, and whilst the RL they were travelling in crossed a dam wall, the vehicle fell into the water. The weight of their webbing with ammo, grenades, water, etc., pulled them under. Altogether 12 of them lost their lives in this tragic accident: P Chapange, S Dudzirayi, T Manduna, J Mangandura, K Muchato, B Murambiwa, T Ndaza, G Ngorovani, M Nyikadzino, C Ranganayi, E Takawira and M Wunganayi.
Manunure	Tongesayi Callisto	642555		WO2	1st Bn	DOAS	08/08/1977	
Mapfumo	Augustine	649991		Pte	1st Bn	Mrd	04/06/1978	Killed by terrorists. Buried in Lady Stanley Cemetery, Bulawayo. Source: Richard Perry.
Marufu	Gwaze	654735		L Cpl	1st Bn	DOAS	27/12/1978	
Masarakufa	Mashona			Temp/Cpl	1st Bn	Mrd	23/03/1973	Killed by terrorists in the Mount Darwin area, *Op Hurricane*.
Mataga	John	644475		WO2	1st Bn	DOAS	06/07/1979	Died of natural causes. Source: Craig Fourie.
Matebwe	Chitanda	645267		Pte	C Coy, 1st Bn	KIA	08/04/1979	
Mathe	Raphael	645552		L Cpl	1st Bn	DOAS	14/06/1979	Died in a vehicle accident in Urungwe TTL, north of Karoi, *Op Hurricane*. Source: Craig Fourie.
Maworera	Richard	645554		L Cpl	1st Bn	DOAS	28/06/1979	

Surname	Name	Number	Award	Rank	Unit	Status	DoD	Footnotes
Mhuka	Mugara Zakaria	644517		Cpl	K Coy, 1st Bn	DOAS	12/06/1977	
Mleya	George Mathias	644704		Sgt	A Coy, 1st Bn	KOAS	21/02/1979	Buried in Lady Stanley Cemetery, Bulawayo. Source: Richard Perry.
Mpofu	Royal	647122		Pte	C Coy, 1st Bn	DOAS	25/03/1978	
Muchato	Kefasi	R42582		L Cpl	Regt Band, HQ Coy, 1st Bn	KOAS	19/05/1972	Drowned in the Fuller Forest, Matetsi area, west of Wankie. He was 30 years old and is buried in Gutu. Source: Death Notice. Members of the band were deployed on active service, and whilst the RL they were travelling in crossed a dam wall, the vehicle fell into the water. The weight of their webbing with ammo, grenades, water, etc., pulled them under. Altogether 12 of them lost their lives in this tragic accident: P Chapange, S Dudzirayi, T Manduna, J Mangandura, K Muchato, B Murambiwa, T Ndaza, G Ngorovani, M Nyikadzino, C Ranganayi, E Takawira and M Wunganayi.
Muchazorega		R42580		Pte	1st Bn	KIA	14/09/1967	Killed in a CT action, *Op Nickel*. *Masodja*, states that elements of 10 Platoon under Lt Noble were following the tracks of 5 CTs since early on the morning of 05 September. Contact was made at 1300 when a CT was killed and another wounded. Thew wounded man through a grenade, killing Nyika and wounding Pte Pedzisayi. The existing date therefore appears wrong, plus *Op Nickel* officially ended at 0600hrs on 08 September. Shay and Vermaak in *The Silent War* mention that a further African soldier was killed in action in early September 1967, during the final mopping up of the ZIPRA Lithuli Gang who were responsible for the deaths in action of Lt N Smith and CSM H Timitayi.
Mukombo	Davison	R41628		L Cpl/ Act Cpl	1st Bn	KIA	13/08/1967	Died from a gunshot wound in a contact near Inyantue, northern Matabeleland, JOC Wankie, *Op Nickel*. Pte Korani also died in this contact.
Munangwa	Constantine Gora	642671		Sgt	11 Pl, D Coy, 1st Bn	KIA	28/11/1976	Died from gunshot wounds received in a contact in Bikita District, *Op Repulse*, at the age of 34. He is buried in the Kadoma area. Source: Death Notice, which spells surname as Munengwa. See also Ndaza.
Munemo	Poncian	644717		L Cpl	1st Bn	KIA	02/04/1975	Died from multiple gunshot wounds in a contact in the North Eastern border area. Died aged 22. Buried in Hartley. Source: Death Notice.
Muneri	Zacharia	643811		Pte	1st Bn	KOAS	13/12/1975	Died in a vehicle accident at the Lunga River Bridge on the Essexvale Road, at the age of 33. Buried in Zaka. Source: Death Notice. *Masodja* lists Muneri as the surname.
Murambiwa	Benjamin	R43901		Pte	Regt Band, HQ Coy, 1st Bn	KOAS	19/05/1972	Drowned in the Fuller Forest, Matetsi area, west of Wankie. He was 32 years old and is buried in Kwe Kwe. Source: Death Notice. Members of the band were deployed on active service, and whilst the RL they were travelling in crossed a dam wall, the vehicle fell into the water. The weight of their webbing with ammo, grenades, water, etc., pulled them under. Altogether 12 of them lost their lives in this tragic accident: P Chapange, S Dudzirayi, T Manduna, J Mangandura, K Muchato, B Murambiwa, T Ndaza, G Ngorovani, M Nyikadzino, C Ranganayi, E Takawira and M Wunganayi.
Murove	Kumanikwa			Pte	A Coy, 1st Bn	KOAS	11/03/1977	Died in an accident. Source: Craig Fourie.
Musabayane	Elton	R44831		Pte	1st Bn	DOAS	27/04/1972	Died in Bulawayo of septicaemia. He was 18 years old and is buried in Bulawayo. Source: Death Notice.

Surname	Name	Number	Award	Rank	Unit	Status	DoD	Footnotes
Mutasa	Pineal (Mutase Piniel)	645043		L Cpl	Spt Coy, 1st Bn	Mrd	15/10/1979	Murdered by CTs. Source: Craig Fourie.
Mutengani	Samuel	646163		L Cpl	1st Bn	KIA	14/06/1979	Died of wounds received in a contact on 12 June. He was casevaced to Mangula where he died two days later. Source: Craig Fourie.
Mutengizanwa	Never	R44047		Pte	1st Bn	KOAS	21/11/1970	Died from multiple injuries, Grey Street, Bulawayo. He was 25 years old and is buried in Kadoma. He was based at Brady Barracks. Source: Death Notice.
Ncube	Amos Sila	645250		Rct	C Coy, 1st Bn	KOAS	14/02/1976	Died in a vehicle accident, on the Umtali/Ft Victoria road, Bikita, at the age of 21. Based at Methuen Barracks. Source: Death Notice. Buried in Lady Stanley Cemetery, Bulawayo. Source: Richard Perry.
Ncube	Patrick	661155		Pte	C Coy, 1st Bn	DOAS	09/04/1979	
Ncube	Stanley	647576		Pte	1st Bn	DOAS	12/06/1977	
Ndaza	Tshaye	R53936		L Cpl	Regt Band, HQ Coy, 1st Bn	KOAS	19/05/1972	Drowned in the Fuller Forest, Matetsi area, west of Wankie. He was 44 years old and is buried in Lupane. Source: Death Notice. Members of the band were deployed on active service, and whilst the RL they were travelling in crossed a dam wall, the vehicle fell into the water. The weight of their webbing with ammo, grenades, water, etc., pulled them under. Altogether 12 of them lost their lives in this tragic accident: P Chapange, S Dudzirayi, T Manduna, J Mangandura, K Muchato, B Murambiwa, T Ndaza, G Ngorovani, M Nyikadzino, C Ranganayi, E Takawira and M Wunganayi.
Ndaza	Tapson Dube	644514		Cpl	1st Bn	KIA	28/11/1976	Died from gunshot wounds in a contact in Bikita District, *Op Repulse*, at the age of 27. He is buried in the Lupane area. Source: Death Notice. See also Munangwa.
Ndhlovu	Morgan	647573		Pte	B Coy, 1st Bn	DOAS	28/08/1977	
Nemanwa	Isaac Ronny	646066		Pte	1st Bn	KOAS	18/09/1978	Died from friendly fire in an air strike. Source: Craig Fourie.
Newton	See F/note	644159		Pte	1st Bn	KOAS	08/08/1971	This would almost certainly not have been his surname, but his first name - a not uncommon habit back then of clerical "errors." Sadly, we may never know his surname, which is so important in tracing our black soldiers' tribal background.
Ngorovani	Godfrey	R42764		Cpl	Regt Band, A Coy, 1st Bn	KOAS	19/05/1972	Drowned in the Fuller Forest, Matetsi area, west of Wankie. He was 34 years old and is buried in Gokwe. Source: Death Notice. Members of the band were deployed on active service, and whilst the RL they were travelling in crossed a dam wall, the vehicle fell into the water. The weight of their webbing with ammo, grenades, water, etc., pulled them under. Altogether 12 of them lost their lives in this tragic accident: P Chapange, S Dudzirayi, T Manduna, J Mangandura, K Muchato, B Murambiwa, T Ndaza, G Ngorovani, M Nyikadzino, C Ranganayi, E Takawira and M Wunganayi.
Nharo		R44846		Pte	1st Bn	KOAS	09/05/1973	Died from a gunshot wound to the chest, North East operational area. He was 20 years old. Source: Death Notice.
Nkala	Christopher	646995		Pte	D Coy, 1st Bn	Mrd	11/10/1978	Killed whilst on leave.
Nyamayaro	Frederick	646316		Pte	1st Bn	DOAS	16/09/1978	
Nyasala	Enias	R44182		Pte	1st Bn	DOAS	03/07/1972	Died in Bulawayo of malaria. He was 25 years old and is buried in Zwimba. Source: Death Notice.

Surname	Name	Number	Award	Rank	Unit	Status	DoD	Footnotes
Nyikadzino	Marandu	R43724		Pte	Regt Band, HQ Coy, 1st Bn	KOAS	19/05/1972	Drowned in the Fuller Forest, Matetsi area, west of Wankie. He was 30 years old and is buried in Buhera. Source: Death Notice. Members of the band were deployed on active service, and whilst the RL they were travelling in crossed a dam wall, the vehicle fell into the water. The weight of their webbing with ammo, grenades, water, etc., pulled them under. Altogether 12 of them lost their lives in this tragic accident: P Chapange, S Dudzirayi, T Manduna, J Mangandura, K Muchato, B Murambiwa, T Ndaza, G Ngorovani, M Nyikadzino, C Ranganayi, E Takawira and M Wunganayi.
Peirson	Kenneth "Ken"	531		Lt	E Coy, 1st Bn	KOAS	22/08/1967	Killed by friendly fire, in the Tjolotjo area, Matabeleland, *Op Nickel*. He was commanding several ambushes for the ZIPRA Lithuli gang, who were responsible for the deaths of Lt N Smith and CSM Timitayi the previous day. He left an ambush position to investigate firing a short distance away and was sadly mistaken for the enemy.
Phiri	Johanne	647601		Pte	1st Bn	DOAS	27/07/1978	
Ranganayi	Chirambgwa	R42792		Pte	Regt Band, HQ Coy, 1st Bn	KOAS	19/05/1972	Drowned in the Fuller Forest, Matetsi area, west of Wankie, *Op Tangent*. He was 32 years old and is buried in Gutu. Source: Death Notice. Members of the band were deployed on active service, and whilst the RL they were travelling in crossed a dam wall, the vehicle fell into the water. The weight of their webbing with ammo, grenades, water, etc., pulled them under. Altogether 12 of them lost their lives in this tragic accident: P Chapange, S Dudzirayi, T Manduna, J Mangandura, K Muchato, B Murambiwa, T Ndaza, G Ngorovani, M Nyikadzino, C Ranganayi, E Takawira and M Wunganayi.
Rubva	Musikwa [Rubya Musiyiwa]	662147		Pte	D Coy, 1st Bn	DOAS	02/08/1979	
Rungano	Manyangire	640353		Sgt	1st Bn	KIA	03/03/1975	Died in Wankie Hospital from multiple injuries from a landmine explosion. He was 38 years old. Source: Death Notice.
Ruwana	Fanny Kudakwashe	644922		Pte	1st Bn	KIA	08/08/1977	Died of wounds received in an ambush. Source Craig Fourie.
Saltiel	Z	644767		Pte	1st Bn	KIA	02/04/1975	Died of wounds received in a contact. Source: Craig Fourie.
Sanders	Claude Herbert	600469		Pte	1st Bn	DOAS	10/07/1979	Died of natural causes. Source: Craig Fourie.
Severino	Stephen	R45161		Pte	1st Bn	KIA	17/01/1974	Killed by a gunshot wound in a contact, Centenary, *Op Hurricane*, at the age of 26. Buried in Bulawayo. Source: Death Notice.
Shambani	Richard Keni	644277		Cpl	1st Bn	KOAS	06/05/1976	Accidental shooting in the operational area, aged 28 years. Source: Death Notice.
Shati	Jongwe			Cpl	1st Bn	Mrd	06/06/1977	Murdered by CTs. Source: Craig Fourie.
Shereni	Thomas	644939		Sgt	1st Bn	KOAS	19/01/1979	Buried in Lady Stanley Cemetery, Bulawayo. Source: Richard Perry.
Sibanda	Fibion	645730		Pte	1st Bn	KOAS	11/06/1979	Died in a vehicle accident. Source: Craig Fourie.
Sibanda	Petros	645549		Pte	D Coy, 1st Bn	KOAS	22/02/1977	Died in a shooting accident. Source: Craig Fourie.
Smith	Nicholas John "Nick"	590		Lt	1 Pl, A Coy, 1st Bn	KIA	22/08/1967	Died of gunshot wounds received in a contact in Tjolotjo TTL (MJ630070), north Matabeleland, *Op Nickel*. He was based at Metheun Barracks. Born in England, he was 23 years old and is buried in Warren Hills Cemetery, Salisbury. CSM Timitiya killed in the same contact. A Churchill High School old boy, Nick passed out at the Sandhurst Military Academy in the UK.

Surname	Name	Number	Award	Rank	Unit	Status	DoD	Footnotes
Swondo		R43298		Pte	1st Bn	KOAS	17/05/1967	Died in a vehicle accident.
Takawira	Ernest	R64741	Exemplary Service Medal (Post) - 22.12.1972	Col Sgt (Drum Major)	Regt Band, HQ Coy, 1st Bn	KOAS	19/05/1972	Drowned in the Fuller Forest, Matetsi area, west of Wankie. He was 38 years old and is buried in Gutu. Source: Death Notice. Members of the band were deployed on active service, and whilst the RL they were travelling in crossed a dam wall, the vehicle fell into the water. The weight of their webbing with ammo, grenades, water, etc., pulled them under. Altogether 12 of them lost their lives in this tragic accident: P Chapange, S Dudzirayi, T Manduna, J Mangandura, K Muchato, B Murambiwa, T Ndaza, G Ngorovani, M Nyikadzino, C Ranganayi, E Takawira and M Wunganayi.
Timitiya	Havahli	R3063		WO2	1 Pl, A Coy, 1st Bn	KIA	22/08/1967	Died of gunshot wounds reveived in a contact in Tjolotjo TTL (MJ630070), north Matabeleland, *Op Nickel*. He was standing behind a tree firing an MAG when hit. Lt Nick Smith, A Coy OC, was killed in the same contact moments later when he came across to Timitayi. Based at Metheun Barracks, he was 42 years old and is buried in Ft Victoria. He saw active service in a Malaya. Source: Death Notice.
Tongayi	Basilio	646355		Pte	1st Bn	KOAS	02/12/1978	Died in a vehicle accident. Buried in Lady Stanley Cemetery, Bulawayo. Source: Richard Perry and Craig Fourie.
Tshuma	Sayino Runyowa	640142		WO2	1st Bn	Mrd	22/11/1975	Died from gunshot wounds, Mfungo Hills, Nemangwe, Gokwe, at the age of 37. He is buried in Gokwe. Sayino joined 1RAR in 1958, after which his ability and and enthusiasm were reflected in his steady promotion through the ranks to his appointment as Platoon Warrant Officer in 1972. From 1973 to 1975 he acted as the Company Sergeant-Major of JOC Mtoko. Source: Death Notice and Nhowo (RAR journal).
Webber	Godfrey James Glanville "Spider"	781165		2Lt	C Coy, 1st Bn	DOAS	07/09/1977	An Umtali Boys High School old boy.
Wunganayi	Maboko	R43457		Pte	Regt Band, HQ Coy, 1st Bn	KOAS	19/05/1972	Drowned in the Fuller Forest, Matetsi area, west of Wankie. He was 29 years old and is buried in Bikita. Source: Death Notice. Members of the band were deployed on active service, and whilst the RL they were travelling in crossed a dam wall, the vehicle fell into the water. The weight of their webbing with ammo, grenades, water, etc., pulled them under. Altogether 12 of them lost their lives in this tragic accident: P Chapange, S Dudzirayi, T Manduna, J Mangandura, K Muchato, B Murambiwa, T Ndaza, G Ngorovani, M Nyikadzino, C Ranganayi, E Takawira and M Wunganayi.
Zinyemba	Saltiel	644769		Pte	1st Bn	KIA	02/04/1975	Died from gunshot wounds in a contact in the North East border area, at the age of 21. Buried in Gutu. Source: Death Notice.

Chapter 6
Roll of Honour: 2RAR Bush War

Surname	Name	Number	Award	Rank	Unit	Status	DoD	Footnotes
Banga	Thomas	646305		L Cpl	2nd Bn	DOAS	04/10/1977	
Bhere	Eriazere	646343		Pte	C Coy, 2nd Bn	KIA	08/09/1978	Died from gunshot wounds received in a contact, Sengwe TTL, *Op Repulse*. See also M Kwayarira and C Nyathi.
Carr	Anthony John "Tony" "Shorty"	V3130		2Lt	C Coy, 2nd Bn	KIA	17/12/1976	Died from gunshot wounds in a contact, Honde Valley, *Op Thrasher*. Died aged 25. Buried at Warren Hills, Salisbury. Source: Death Notice. He was a school teacher at Vainona High in Salisbury. A Hamilton High School old boy. See also D Sidambe.
Chaka	T. (I.?)			Pte	2nd Bn	DOAS	03/08/1979	
Chaputika	Jerifanosi	645914		L Cpl	2nd Bn	DOAS	26/11/1979	
Chikozho	Michael	646432		Pte	2nd Bn	Mrd	24/07/1977	Killed by terrorists.
Chioneso	Peter	662343		Pte	2nd Bn	DOAS	22/12/1979	
Chirau	Claudious	660903		Pte	A Coy, 2nd Bn	DOAS	10/09/1978	
Chirwa	Isaac	660774		Pte	D Coy, 2nd Bn	DOAS	06/08/1979	
Choto	Cletos	647410		Cpl	2nd Bn	DOAS	25/02/1980	Asphyxia
Dennison	André	781030	MLM - 23.09.77 BCR - 09.02.79 MFC (Ops) - 31.3.1978. See F/note	Maj	CO, A Coy, 2nd Bn	KOAS	03/06/1979	Killed by friendly fire. Dennison and others were in the pub of the Zimbabwe Ruins Hotel when it came under CT attack. He reacted with two others from RAR and two from BSAP. One of the policemen heard a noise in front of him and opened fire, hitting Dennison. He was awarded the BCR, as a result of his actions in a contact in October 1978. Despite having a shattered femur and bleeding heavily, he refused to be casevaced and continued to direct the fight. His bravery and dedication was far beyond the normal call of duty. His MFC (Ops) was for dragging a wounded comrade, under heavy fire, out of a cave where a CT had established himself. Source: Contact 2.
Dube	Stanford	646478		Pte	2nd Bn	KIA	01/03/1977	Killed In a contact.
Dzimba	Fibion	646192		Pte	2nd Bn	KOAS	31/07/1977	Buried in Mbalabala.
Erekan (Erikani)	Richard	660853		Pte	2nd Bn	DOAS	20/11/1978	
Goko	Felix	647457		Pte	2nd Bn	KIA	22/12/1979	Died of shrapnel wounds received in a CT action. Source: Craig Fourie.
Hungwe	Emerson	647997		Pte	2nd Bn	DOAS	08/04/1979	
Jakata	Isaac	643690		Pte	2nd Bn	DOAS	13/06/77	

Surname	Name	Number	Award	Rank	Unit	Status	DoD	Footnotes
John - not his surname	M	645300		Cpl	2nd Bn	DOAS	07/07/1979	Pronounced dead in terms of the Missing Persons Act. Source: Craig Fourie. This would almost certainly not have been his surname, but his first name - a not uncommon habit back then of clerical "errors." Sadly, we may never know his surname, which is so important in tracing our black soldiers' tribal background.
Kanjani	Michael	661417		Pte	A Coy, 2nd Bn	KIA	12/11/1979	Died of gunshot wounds received in a CT action. Source: Craig Fourie.
Kurebwa	Tarirayi	648005		Pte	2nd Bn	DOAS	14/10/1977	
Kwami	Marko			Pte	2nd Bn	DOAS	21/01/1979	
Kwayarira	Maphios	660408		Pte	C Coy, 2nd Bn	KIA	08/09/1978	Died from gunshot wounds in a contact, Sengwe TTL, *Op Repulse*. See also E Bhere and C Nyathi.
Mabhena	A.			Pte	2nd Bn	DOAS	01/12/1977	Source: Craig Fourie.
Madziviridzo	Denny	661615		Pte	2nd Bn	DOAS	30/06/1978	
Magonda	Peter	648069		Pte	2nd Bn	KIA	22/11/1979	Died from gunshot wounds received in a CT action. Source: Craig Fourie.
Mahogo	Charles	646356		Pte	2nd Bn	KOAS	12/07/1976	Died from an accidental gunshot wound to the head, Ft Victoria, *Op Repulse*. He was 19 years old. Source: Death Notice.
Makoni	Boniface	662205		Pte	2nd Bn	DOAS	06/02/1980	Died of a subdural haemorrhage. Source: Craig Fourie.
Manunure	Patrick (Phillip?)	646896		Pte	2nd Bn	Mrd	13/08/1977	Killed whilst on leave.
Manyika	Christopher	662508		Pte	2nd Bn	DOAS	02/04/1979	
Marova	Francis	645997		L Cpl	A Coy, 2nd Bn	KIA	12/04/1978	Killed by a gunshot wound to the head when surprised by two ZANLA in a contact north of Mrewa , *Op Hurricane*. He succeeded in killing a CT before he died. Source: Craig Fourie.
Marufu	Freddy	648036		Pte	2nd Bn	DOAS	19/03/1979	
Marufu	J.			Cpl	2nd Bn	DOAS	09/07/1979	
Mashona	Masarakufa			Cpl	2nd Bn	DOAS	24/03/1977	
Matavire	Maxwell	647515		Pte	C Coy, 2nd Bn	KIA	17/08/1978	Died from gunshot wounds in a contact, Matibi 2 TTL, *Op Repulse*.
Mlalazi	Patrick	648073		Pte	Spt Coy, 2nd Bn	DOAS	08/08/1977	Died in a vehicle accident. Source: Craig Fourie.
Moyo	Canaan (K)	647489		L Cpl	2nd Bn	KIA	22/12/1979	Died from shrapnel wounds received in a CT action. Source: Craig Fourie.
Moyo	D.	645726		Pte	2nd Bn	KOAS	06/01/1977	Died in a vehicle accident.
Moyo	Rodwell	646048		Cpl	A Coy, 2nd Bn	DOAS	10/04/1979	
Moyo	Tamusanga Clever	660414		Pte	A Coy, 2nd Bn	KIA	09/03/1979	Killed by a mortar bomb, *Op Repulse*. See also Notice Sibanda.

Surname	Name	Number	Award	Rank	Unit	Status	DoD	Footnotes
Mpofu	Leonard	649979		Pte	A Coy, 2nd Bn	KIA	27/06/1978	Killed by a gunshot wound.
Mucheka	Tadios			Pte	2nd Bn	DOAS	17/04/1977	
Muchemwa	S. Marufu	644539		Sgt	A Coy, 2nd Bn	KOAS	20/01/1977	Died in a vehicle accident en route to Ft Victoria. Source: Craig Fourie. Listed in *Contact* under Marufu.
Mudzingi	Ruben			Pte	2nd Bn	DOAS	27/02/1979	
Mujere	Levy	647540		Pte	2nd Bn	DOAS	07/12/1978	
Mukandatsama	Munikwi	645534		Pte	C Coy, 2nd Bn	KIA	28/02/1979	Died from gunshot wounds in a contact in Ndanga TTL, Zaka, *Op Repulse*.
Mukapanda	Aaron	647516		Pte	2nd Bn	DOAS	05/11/1977	
Munyorwa	Gift	647478		L Cpl	D Coy, 2nd Bn	DOAS	03/05/1979	
Musindo	Maxwell (E?)	648028		Pte	4th Pl 2nd Bn	DOAS	10/03/1979	
Mutamburi	Killian			Pte	Spt Coy, 2nd Bn	KOAS	09/12/1979	Source: Craig Fourie.
Mutargoza	Toperson	646018		Act L Cpl	A Coy, 2nd Bn	KIA	29/12/1977	Killed by a gunshot wound when his vehicle was ambushed by 30 ZANLA in the Mshawasha African Purchase Area just south of Ft Victoria, *Op Repulse*. See also C Ngomanyoni.
Mutema	Tinarwo	646312		Pte	B Coy, 2nd Bn	KOAS	03/05/1977	Died in a vehicle accident. Source: Craig Fourie.
Muzingi	Reuben	647532		Pte	B Coy, 2nd Bn	DOAS	27/02/1979	
Mviyo	Masungwa Tobias	644546		Pte	8 Pl, C Coy, 2nd Bn	KIA	05/05/1976	Died from a gunshot wound, Ruda, Honde Valley, Mutasa District, *Op Thrasher*, at the age of 24. He is buried in Zaka. Source: Death Notice. Contact lists same service number and date, but gives his unit as 2 Rhodesia Regiment which, at that time, is unlikely.
Mweneziko	Mudzingwa	644740		Sgt	2nd Bn	DOAS	25/10/1978	
Ngomanyoni	Crispen	646067		L Cpl	A Coy, 2nd Bn	KIA	29/12/1977	Killed by a gunshot wound when his vehicle was ambushed by 30 ZANLA in the Mshawasha African Purchase Area. See also T Mutargoza.
Ngulube	Isaac	646059		Cpl	A Coy, 2nd Bn	KIA	05/08/1978	Died of wounds received in a contact, *Op Repulse*. Source: Craig Fourie.
Ngwenya	Abednigo			Pte	Spt Coy, 2nd Bn	DOAS	10/09/1978	
Rujada	Honda			L Cpl	2nd Bn	DOAS	16/03/1978	
Runodada	Chibomba	644239		Pte	C Coy, 2nd Bn	KIA	28/02/1979	Died of wounds received in an ambush. Source Craig Fourie.
Sengu	Elaja	648150		Pte	2nd Bn	DOAS	05/09/1977	

Surname	Name	Number	Award	Rank	Unit	Status	DoD	Footnotes
Shereni	Peter	644678		Cpl	A Coy, 2nd Bn	KIA	22/12/1976	Died from shrapnel wounds received in a mortar attack, Matibi TTL, *Op Repulse*, at the age of 24.
Sibanda	Notice (Nickson)	661746		Pte	A Coy, 2nd Bn	KIA	09/03/1979	Killed by a mortar bomb, *Op Repulse*. See also Tamusanga Moyo.
Sidambe	Dennis (Also Kenneth)	647020		Pte	C Coy, 2nd Bn	KIA	17/12/1976	Died from gunshot wounds in a contact, Honde Valley, *Op Thrasher*, at the age of 16. He was based in Ft Victoria and is buried in Bulawayo. Source: Death Notice. See also A Carr.
Tarusari	Julius	644091		Pte	2nd Bn	KOAS	23/10/1976	Died in a vehicle accident.
Tauya	David	644751		Pte	2nd Bn	KOAS	03/05/1977	Died in a vehicle accident. Source: Craig Fourie.
Tavugara	Murira	644772		T Cpl	C Coy, 2nd Bn	KIA	04/06/1976	Died in Salisbury Hospital from shrapnel wounds. He was 23 years old. Source: Death Notice.
Thompson	Bruce Malcolm	781139	SCR (Post) - 13.10.78. See F/note	2LT	A Coy, 2nd Bn	KIA	27/06/1978	Killed by a gunshot wound. His SCR citation states that he was involved in 35 contacts in which 170 CTs were killed. This included 29 parachute deployments. In a contact on 27 June 1978, under very heavy fire, he went to the rescue of his wounded machine gunner. He accounted for 2 CTs, but in the follow up he was fatally shot. (Source: *Masodja*) Former teacher at St Stephen's college, Balla Balla. An Umtali Boys High School old boy.
Totohwiyo	Lovemore	660798		Pte	2nd Bn	KOAS	29/12/1978	
Tshababa	Dick			Pte	2nd Bn	KOAS	06/01/1977	Died in a vehicle accident. Source: Craig Fourie.
Turusari	Julian Chinaka	646091		Pte	2nd Bn	KOAS	23/10/1976	Died from a gunshot wound in the operational area. He was 21 years old. Source: Death Notice.
Tuzayi (Tutayi?)	Boniface	648153		Pte	2nd Bn	DOAS	08/04/1978	
Zinyakatiri	Onias	648169		Pte	2nd Bn	DOAS	15/01/1978	

Chapter 7

Roll of Honour: 3RAR and Independent Companies Bush War

Surname	Name	No.	Award	Rank	Unit	Status	DoD	Footnotes
Bicknell	Kevin Howard	113536		Sgt	3 Pl 1(Indep) Coy	KOAS	10/04/1978	Died of gunshot wounds sustained in a shooting incident at the Essexvale Battle Camp, *Op Tangent*. Upon returning from R&R on that Monday, twenty members of this Company had drawn rifles and live ammunition for retraining purposes. They assembled at the end of a football field, where they stripped their weapons for cleaning prior to moving to the rifle range for firing practice. Once the group had stripped their FNs, a Pte Robert Nyamini Mapfumo suddenly cocked his rifle and opened fire on automatic at his fellow soldiers. As Mapfumo's 20-round magazine emptied, and before he could replace it with a fully charged one, Privates Mawonda and Zevezene overpowered and disarmed Mapfumo. Tragically though, four lay dead and four were seriously wounded. Cpl Stephen Randall of Bulawayo, L Cpl Michael Wall of Que Que, Sgt Kevin Bicknell of Hartley and Pte John Tshuma of Bembesi had lost their lives. Sgt Vic Anderson, Cpl Malcolm Partridge, L Cpl Rob Garitzio and Pte David Chiremba had been wounded. In spite of claiming insanity, Mapfumo was found guilty of murder in the High Court in Bulawayo and sentenced to death. Also found listed as 4 (Indep) Coy and DoD as 19 April, but first-hand accounts confirm that these details are incorrect. Source: Andrew Barrett. Intake 155 DRR. A Prince Edward School old boy.
Carroll	Tony Charles	114666		Cpl	3(Indep) Coy	KIA	04/06/1978	Killed in a contact, *Op Thrasher*. An Umtali Boys High School old boy.
Cerff	Robert Hugh "Rob"	106161		Cpl	3(Indep) Coy	KIA	18/03/1978	Operating from the old police camp in Nyamaropa, *Op Thrasher*, a stick of four encountered a very large group of CTs. In the ensuing engagement, and in spite of Cpl Cerff's desperate pleas for help over the radio, the stick was overrun and only the MAG gunner, having run out of ammunition, managed to escape, returning to base a couple of days later. Cpl Rob Cerff and Privates Elson Makonde and Jacob Nkomo were all killed. Source Rod McLean who was in Nyamaropa at the time. A Gifford High School old boy.
Chilenje	Samuel	662021		Pte	1(Indep) Coy	KOAS	29/11/1978	Died aged 17. Buried in the Athlone Cemetery, Bulawayo. Source: Richard Perry.
Chinduma	Pondai	649372		Pte	2 Pl 3(Indep) Coy	KOAS	19/02/1979	Died from gunshot wounds in an ambush near Avila Mission, in the Ruwangwe area, north of Inyanga, *Op Thrasher*. Des Washington and Pondai Chinduma were killed in the contact and two badly wounded. Source Gary Thomson who was in the same contact.
Chipo	Jetro	649229		Pte	2(Indep) Coy	DOAS	12/01/1979	
Chipondera	Same			Pte	6(Indep) Coy	DOAS	19/03/1980	
Chivisi	Tamba	649194		Pte	2(Indep) Coy	DOAS	21/01/1979	
du Toit	Andrew Jameson "Gus"	V5047		2LT	3(Indep) Coy	KIA	27/12/1979	Killed in a CT action. A Prince Edward School old boy.

Surname	Name	No.	Award	Rank	Unit	Status	DoD	Footnotes
Fairbanks	Peter Hendrik J.	110590		L Cpl	5(Indep) Coy	KIA	02/09/1978	Killed in the Chipinga district, *Op Thrasher*. A farmer from Gazaland. An Umtali Boys High School old boy.
Hartley	Edward James	124628		Rfn	6(Indep) Coy	KIA	12/10/1978	Killed in a contact in the *Op Thrasher* area. A Marandellas High School old boy.
Hussey	Godfrey Kenneth	110016		Rfn	4(Indep) Coy	DOAS	27/04/1978	Died in a vehicle accident near Milibizi, *Op Tangent*. Intake 155 DRR. A Hamilton Hogh School old boy.
Kelly	Michael David	81145		Sgt	3(Indep) Coy	KOAS	04/06/1978	Killed in shooting incident in the *Op Thrasher* area. A Guinea Fowl School old boy.
Khanye	George	648867		Pte	2(Indep) Coy	KOAS	22/10/1979	Died in a vehicle accident.
Khupe	Jenamiso	648897		Pte	5(Indep) Coy	KIA	12/05/1978	Killed in a contact, at the age of 24. Buried in Lady Stanley Cemetery, Bulawayo. Source: Richard Perry.
Machore	K.	649175		Pte	2(Indep) Coy	DOAS	09/03/1979	
Makonde	Elson	648811		Pte	3(Indep) Coy	KIA	18/03/1978	Operating from the old police camp in Nyamaropa, *Op Thrasher*, a stick of four encountered a very large group of CTs. In the ensuing engagement, and in spite of Cpl Cerff's desperate pleas for help over the radio, the stick was overrun and only the MAG gunner, having run out of ammunition, managed to escape, returning to base a couple of days later. Cpl Rob Cerff and Privates Elson Makonde and Jacob Nkomo were all killed. Source Rod McLean who was in Nyamaropa at the time. Buried in Lady Stanley Cemetery, Bulawayo. Source: Richard Perry.
Matthews	Grant Stewart	107475		Rfn	1(Indep) Coy	KIA	09/12/1979	Died from wounds in a CT action in Fort Victoria, *Op Repulse*. Killed in the same incident as Phinias Mpofu.
Meyer	Victor Carl	98858		Cpl	1(Indep) Coy	KOAS	19/03/1979	Died in a drowning accident on the Zambezi river. Victor's stick was ordered to OP an arms cache on an island downstream from Victoria Falls but, after several days of inactivity his 2Lt decided to swim to the island for an inspection. Victor made it to the island only to realise his officer was in difficulty and returned to the water to save the officer's life - which he did but, lost his own in the process. His body was never found and, in the plethora of admin and investigations, it is possible that Vic was overlooked for a bravery award.
Mpofu	Phinias	649609		Pte	1(Indep) Coy	KIA	09/12/1979	Killed in a CT action in Fort Victoria, *Op Repulse*. Killed in the same incident as Grant Matthews.
Muchore	K.	649175		Pte	2(Indep) Coy	DOAS	09/03/1979	
Murdock	Timothy Joseph "Tim"	118553		L Cpl	1 Pl 3(Indep) Coy	KIA	28/11/1978	Killed in an ambush, Inyanga, *Op Thrasher*. Source: Andrew Dorking, fiancé of Timothy's sister, Julia. They were escorting sticks back from Nyamaropa when the truck hit a landmine, followed by an ambush from about 200 metres away. Tim was the MAG gunner. Source: Gary Thomson. An Allan Wilson High School old boy.
Mutanga	Mastaff	649775		Pte	2(Indep) Coy	KIA	23/01/1979	Died from wounds received in a contact near Karoi, *Op Hurricane*. He was casevaced to Kariba where he subsequently died. Source: Craig Fourie.
Nel	Pieter Jacobus Stephanus "Piet"	119582		Sgt	6(Indep) Coy	KOAS	16/06/1979	Killed whilst trying to disarm an RPG rocket, Inyanga, *Op Thrasher*. The rocket was to be kept for a souvenir but, it exploded and killed him instantly in the barrack room. Source: Andre Barlow. Also found listed as 3 (Indep) Coy. Died at the age of 21. His headstone gives his unit as 6 Indep Coy RAR. He is buried in the Umtali Cemetery.

Surname	Name	No.	Award	Rank	Unit	Status	DoD	Footnotes
Nkomo	Jacob	649246		Pte	3(Indep) Coy	KIA	18/03/1978	Operating from the old police camp in Nyamaropa, *Op Thrasher*, a stick of four encountered a very large group of CTs. In the ensuing engagement, and in spite of Cpl Cerff's desperate pleas for help over the radio, the stick was overrun and only the MAG gunner, having run out of ammunition, managed to escape, returning to base a couple of days later. Cpl Rob Cerff and Privates Elson Makonde and Jacob Nkomo were all killed. Source Rod McLean who was in Nyamaropa at the time. Buried in Lady Stanley Cemetery, Bulawayo. Source: Richard Perry.
Ntindindi	J.	650061		Pte	6(Indep) Coy	DOAS	05/04/1978	
Nyoni	A	649326		Pte	1(Indep) Coy	KOAS	29/11/1978	Died aged 28. Buried in Lady Stanley Cemetery, Bulawayo. Source: Richard Perry.
Pasina	Robert	649610		Pte	1(Indep) Coy	KIA	03/10/1979	Killed in a CT action. DoD of 12 Oct also found.
Randall	Stephen William	114232		L Cpl	1(Indep) Coy	KOAS	10/04/1978	Died of gunshot wounds sustained in a shooting incident at the Essexvale Battle Camp, *Op Tangent*. Upon returning from R&R on that Monday, twenty members of this Company had drawn rifles and live ammunition for retraining purposes. They assembled at the end of a football field, where they stripped their weapons for cleaning prior to moving to the rifle range for firing practice. Once the group had stripped their FNs, a Pte Robert Nyamini Mapfumo suddenly cocked his rifle and opened fire on automatic at his fellow soldiers. As Mapfumo's 20-round magazine emptied, and before he could replace it with a fully charged one, Privates Mawonda and Zevezene overpowered and disarmed Mapfumo. Tragically though, four lay dead and four were seriously wounded. Cpl Stephen Randall of Bulawayo, L Cpl Michael Wall of Kwe Kwe, Sgt Kevin Bicknell of Hartley and Pte John Tshuma of Bembesi had lost their lives. Sgt Vic Anderson, Cpl Malcolm Partridge, L Cpl Rob Garitzio and Pte David Chiremba had been wounded. In spite of claiming insanity, Mapfumo was found guilty of murder in the High Court in Bulawayo and sentenced to death. Also found listed as 4 (Indep) Coy and DoD as 19 April, but first-hand accounts confirm that these details are incorrect. Source: Andrew Barrett. A Milton High School old boy.
Rutunga	Phineas M.	648580		Pte	5(Indep) Coy	DOAS	13/05/1978	
Tshuma	Johani	649222		Pte	1(Indep) Coy	KOAS	10/04/1978	Died of gunshot wounds sustained in a shooting incident at the Essexvale Battle Camp, *Op Tangent*. Upon returning from R&R on that Monday, twenty members of this Company had drawn rifles and live ammunition for retraining purposes. They assembled at the end of a football field, where they stripped their weapons for cleaning prior to moving to the rifle range for firing practice. Once the group had stripped their FNs, a Pte Robert Nyamini Mapfumo suddenly cocked his rifle and opened fire on automatic at his fellow soldiers. As Mapfumo's 20-round magazine emptied, and before he could replace it with a fully charged one, Privates Mawonda and Zevezene overpowered and disarmed Mapfumo. Tragically though, four lay dead and four were seriously wounded. Cpl Stephen Randall of Bulawayo, L Cpl Michael Wall of Kwe Kwe, Sgt Kevin Bicknell of Hartley and Pte John Tshuma of Bembesi had lost their lives. Sgt Vic Anderson, Cpl Malcolm Partridge, L Cpl Rob Garitzio and Pte David Chiremba had been wounded. In spite of claiming insanity, Mapfumo was found guilty of murder in the High Court in Bulawayo and sentenced to death. Also found listed as 4 (Indep) Coy and DoD as 19 April, but first-hand accounts confirm that these details are incorrect. Source: Andrew Barrett.

Surname	Name	No.	Award	Rank	Unit	Status	DoD	Footnotes
Wall	Michael Anthony	118425		L Cpl	1(Indep) Coy	KOAS	10/04/1978	Died of gunshot wounds sustained in a shooting incident at the Essexvale Battle Camp, *Op Tangent*. Upon returning from R&R on that Monday, twenty members of this Company had drawn rifles and live ammunition for retraining purposes. They assembled at the end of a football field, where they stripped their weapons for cleaning prior to moving to the rifle range for firing practice. Once the group had stripped their FNs, a Pte Robert Nyamini Mapfumo suddenly cocked his rifle and opened fire on automatic at his fellow soldiers. As Mapfumo's 20-round magazine emptied, and before he could replace it with a fully charged one, Privates Mawonda and Zevezene overpowered and disarmed Mapfumo. Tragically though, four lay dead and four were seriously wounded. Cpl Stephen Randall of Bulawayo, L Cpl Michael Wall of Kwe Kwe, Sgt Kevin Bicknell of Hartley and Pte John Tshuma of Bembesi had lost their lives. Sgt Vic Anderson, Cpl Malcolm Partridge, L Cpl Rob Garitzio and Pte David Chiremba had been wounded. In spite of claiming insanity, Mapfumo was found guilty of murder in the High Court in Bulawayo and sentenced to death. Also found listed as 4 (Indep) Coy and DoD as 19 April, but first-hand accounts confirm that these details are incorrect. Source: Andrew Barrett. A Kwe Kwe High School old boy.
Washington	Desmond Kenneth "Des"	123353		Rfn	2 Pl 3(Indep) Coy	KIA	19/02/1979	Died from gunshot wounds in an ambush near Avila Mission, in the Ruwangwe area, north of Inyanga, *Op Thrasher*. Intake 163. Des Washington and Pondai Chinduma were killed in the contact and two badly wounded. Source Gary Thomson who was in the same contact. An Ellis Robins High School old boy.
Zimuna	F.	963849		L Cpl	4(Indep) Coy	DOAS	08/10/1978	

Other

Surname	Name	Number	Award	Rank	Unit	Status	DoD	Footnotes
Chitiyo	Benjamin	647427		Rct	Depot	KOAS	01/11/1976	Accidental shooting, Umzingwane area, *Op Tangent*. He was 19 years old. Source: Death Notice.
Govo	D.	665337		Pte	Depot	KOAS	07/09/1979	Died of gunshot wounds. Source: Craig Fourie.
Hlabiso	L.	648526		Rct	Depot	DOAS	14/10/1977	
Magogo	R.			Rct	Depot	DOAS	01/05/1977	Died of natural causes, *Op Tangent*. Source: Craig Fourie.
Makutukira	A	661425		Pte	Depot	DOAS	09/05/1978	
Muchenje	Raphael	647507		Rct	Depot	KOAS	25/12/1976	Died in Binga Hospital from severe injuries he sustained when he fell off a cliff. He was 26 years old. Source: Death Notice.
Shabani	Thembikile Bubi	662465		Rct	Depot	DOAS	11/02/1979	
Sibanda	Raphael S.	662177		Rct	Depot	KOAS	08/06/1979	Died aged 17. Buried in Lady Stanley Cemetery, Bulawayo. Source: Richard Perry.
Sibanda	Robert	651106		Pte	C Coy, 10th Bn RR	KIA	16/04/1979	Died from gunshot wounds in a CT action, at the age of 23. Buried in the Athlone Cemetery, Bulawayo. His headstone carries a large RAR badge, but also carries the inscription 10RR. Source: Richard Perry and Craig Fourie.
Sibanda	T.	649901		Pte	3rd Bn	KOAS	14/03/1980	Died from a gunshot wound. Source: Craig Fourie. Umtali based Brigade.

Bibliography

Binda, A., *Masodja*, 30 Degrees South Publishing, Newlands, 2007

Capell, Lt-Col A.E., *The 2nd Rhodesia Regiment in East Africa*, The Naval and Military Press, Uckfield, 2008

Commonwealth War Graves Commission: http://www.cwgc.org/

Gibbs, P. & Phillips, H., *The History of the British South Africa Police*, Something of Value, Melbourne, 2000

Haggett, A. & van Tonder, G.R., *Rhodesian Combined Forces Roll of Honour 1966–1981,* 30 Degrees South Publishing, Pinetown, 2012

Harding, Col C. CMG, DSO, *Frontier Patrols*

London Gazette: Archives

Lovett, J., *Contact*, Galaxie Press, Salisbury, 1977

Lucas, Sir C., KCB, KCMG (ed.), *The Empire at War, Volume IV*, Oxford University Press, 1921

McLean, R. South Africa War Graves Project: http://www.southafricawargraves.org/

McLaughlin, P., *Ragtime Soldiers; the Rhodesian experience in the First World War*, Books of Zimbabwe, Bulawayo, 1980

Moorcraft, P., *Contact II*, Sygma, Johannesburg, 1981

National Archives (UK), Medal Index Cards

National Archives (UK), *Official History: Military Operations East Africa*. Volume I. August 1914–September 1916

National Archives (UK), *Official History: Military Operations East Africa*. Draft Chapter XII to the unpublished Volume 1

Rogers, C.E., (collated) *1st Rhodesia Native Regiment – some reminiscences, by Lt-Col A.J. Tomlinson, Commanding Officer,* from a series of articles published in the Rhodesian Defence Force Journal from May 1919 to September 1920

Saffery, D., *Rhodesia Medal Roll: Honours and Decorations of the Rhodesian Conflict, 1970–1981*, Jeppestown Press, Johannesburg, 2006

Shay, R. & Vermaak, C., *The Silent War*, Galaxie Press, Salisbury, 1971

Stapleton, T.J., *No Insignificant Part. The Rhodesia Native Regiment and the East Africa Campaign of the First World War*, Wilfrid Laurier University Press, Waterloo, 2005

Wall, D., *Insignia and History of the Rhodesian Armed Forces 1890-1980*, Just Done, Durban, 2005

Wright, T., *The History of the Northern Rhodesia Police*, British Empire & Commonwealth Museum, Bristol, 2001

Appendix 1

Regimental Song

In February 1942, the newly formed regimental band of the Rhodesian African Rifles made the first of thousands of public appearances; displays that would forever endear the magic of their music and awe-inspiring vocal harmonies with the Rhodesian public.

Later that year, in a competition four African songs were selected, from which to come up with a suitable regimental march arrangement. The final song recounted stories of a regiment on the march, but the well-known *Sweet Banana,* synonymous with the men of the RAR, was to evolve during WWII when the battalion was in South Africa escorting Italians POWs in South Africa's Natal Province. At every stop on their train journeys, locals would hawk cheap, tasty bananas to the troops.

Although the original words would change with time, from references to railway stations in Natal to combat theatres of war that the battalion fought in, the chorus, delivered with faultless harmony, endured, '*Banana, Banana, I will buy you a sweet banana*'.

The lyrics shown are in the chiShona and isiNdebele languages, with the English version on the right:

Verse 1

A,B,C,D,E, Headquarter	A,B,C,D,E, Headquarter
Siyakutengera sweet banana	I will buy you a sweet banana
A,B,C,D,E, Headquarter	A,B,C,D,E, Headquarter
Siyakuthengeli sweet banana	I will buy you a sweet banana
Banana, banana, banana	Banana, banana, banana
Banana, banana	Banana, banana
Siyakuthengeli sweet banana	I will buy you a sweet banana

Chorus

Nhowo, Pfumo ne tsvimbo	Shield, spear and knobkerrie
Ndiyo RAR, muhondo ne runyararo	That's RAR, in war and peace
Ndichakutengera sweet banana	I will buy you a sweet banana

Verse 2

Burma, Egypt ne Malaya	Burma, Egypt and Malaya
Takarwa tikakunda	We fought and we conquered
Federation ne Rhodesia	The Federation and Rhodesia
Takarwa tikakunda	We fought and we conquered
Muhondo, muhondo, muhondo	In war, in war, in war
Muhondo RAR, inorwa nokushinga	In war she fights with bravery

Chorus

Verse 3

One, Two, Depot RAR	One, Two, Depot RAR
Ndidzo dzichapedza hondo dzose	They will finish all wars
One, Two, Depot RAR	One, Two, Depot RAR
Ndidzo dzichapedza hondo dzose	They will finish all wars
Banana, banana, banana	Banana, banana, banana
Banana, banana	Banana, banana
Ndichakutengera sweet banana	I will buy you a sweet banana

Chorus

Verse 4

A,B,C,D, Support, Headquarter	A,B,C,D, Support, Headquarter
Ndichakutengera sweet banana	I will buy you a sweet banana
A,B,C,D, Support, Headquarter	A,B,C,D, Support, Headquarter
Ndichakutengera sweet banana	I will buy you a sweet banana
Banana, banana, banana	Banana, banana, banana
Banana, banana	Banana, banana
Ndichakutengera sweet banana	I will buy you a sweet banana

Appendix 11

Honours and Awards RNR

Victoria Cross (VC)
For gallantry
8 June 1917
Sergeant Frederick Charles Francis BOOTH, DCM
Citation: *"For most conspicuous bravery during an attack, in thick bush, on an enemy position. Under very heavy rifle fire, Sjt Booth went forward alone and brought in a man who was dangerously wounded. Later, he rallied native troops, who were badly disorganized, and brought them to the firing line. This NCO has on many previous occasions displayed the greatest bravery, coolness and resourcefulness in action, and has set a splendid example of pluck, endurance and determination."*

Officer of the Order of the British Empire (Mil) (OBE)
For service to the Empire
Major George James THORNTON

Member of the Order of the British Empire (Mil) (MBE)
For service to the Empire
07 February 1919
Lieutenant Francis Arthur HOPKINS
Special List
"The KING has been graciously pleased to give orders for the following appointments to the Most Excellent Order of the British Empire, for valuable services rendered in connection with military operations in East Africa. Dated 1st January, 1919: To be Members of the Military Division of the said Most Excellent Order:"

Military Cross (MC)
For gallantry during active operations against the enemy
26 April 1917
Lieutenant Harry Thomas ONYETT
Citation: *"For conspicuous gallantry and devotion to duty. With a small party, he captured an enemy entrenched position held by 150 rifles and three machine guns."*

1 January 1918
Temporary Lieutenant Charles GREY

Distinguished Conduct Medal (DCM)
For gallantry in the field
3 May 1917
Sergeant Frederick Charles Francis BOOTH
Citation: *"For conspicuous gallantry on many occasions. He showed a splendid example of courage and good leadership, inspiring confidence in his men. He twice carried dispatches through enemy lines."*

Sergeant LITA
Citation: *"For conspicuous gallantry in action on many occasions. His example and influence with his men is incalculable."*

Military Medal (MM)
For acts of gallantry and devotion to duty under fire
26 May 1917
"His Majesty the KING has been graciously pleased to award the Military Medal for bravery in the Field to the undermentioned Non-Commissioned Officers and Men:"
Warrant Officer Class I William Diddons BAKER
Company Sergeant Major Charles M.W. CRAXTON
Sergeant Francis Charles EDWARDS
Sergeant SALIMA

13 March 1918
Sergeant Ronald C. NORTHCOTE
Citation: *"For conspicuous gallantry in action at the Mpepo-Ruhudje River on 19 August 1917. This NCO displayed great coolness and courage, and brought in a wounded askari under fire from enemy trenches."*
Corporal NSUGA
Citation: *"For conspicuous gallantry in action at Likassa near Mpepo-Ruhudje on 30 August 1917. During the action this NCO and his officer were both wounded. Cpl Nsuga's wound was slight but that suffered by Lt Booth was sufficiently severe to prevent his getting away without assistance. Cpl Nsuga remained with Lt Booth and helped him away, thus preventing the latter from falling into enemy hands."*

Mentioned in Dispatches
Commanders in the field submitted periodical reports to the commander-in-chief, which were known as dispatches. These would sometimes contain names of officers and men whose actions significantly contributed to the campaign, for the commanding general's consideration. Those 'mentioned in dispatches' after 1914 were awarded with oak leaf insignia to be attached to the campaign medal ribbon.

25 September 1917
Brigadier-General Edward NORTHEY ADC
Commanding, Nyasaland-Rhodesia Force, East Africa
"The list of recommendations for award or mention in despatches which I now have the honour to submit covers a period of arduous campaigning extending over seventeen months, no such recommendations having been made from this force since 11th October, 1915."
[Author's note: These are listed in the London Gazette as 1st Rhodesia Regiment, which is obviously incorrect as that regiment did not serve in East Africa]

Sergeant Noel ARNOTT
Temporary Lieutenant William James BAKER (KIA 29 March 1917)
Sergeant William Diddons BAKER
Sergeant Frederick Charles Francis BOOTH, VC, DCM
Temporary Major Clive Lancaster CARBUTT

Temporary Second Lieutenant William John CARR
Private CHINGINGO
Sergeant Charles M.W. CRAXTON
Corporal DADA
Sergeant Francis Charles EDWARDS, MM
Sergeant Francis Arthur HOPKINS
Sergeant LITA DCM
Private MGWAGWA
Temporary Lieutenant William Frederick Croei MORGANS
Sergeant SALIMA MM
Sergeant Lawrence Charles SYMONS

07 March 1918
Brigadier-General Edward Northey CB, ADC
Commanding, Nyasaland-Rhodesia Force, East Africa
"I have the honour to submit the subjoined names for mentions in despatches."
Major Francis Hallowes ADDISON
Temporary Lieutenant Frederick Charles Francis BOOTH VC, DCM
Private NDARIMANI
Captain Francis John WANE

06 August 1918
War Office, 6th August 1918, East Africa:
"The names of the undermentioned have been brought to the notice of the Secretary of State for War by Lieutenant-General. Sir J. L. van Deventer, KCB, Commanding-in-Chief, British Forces East Africa, for distinguished services during the operations from 30th May to December, 1917, described in his despatch of 21st January, 1918:"
Temporary Second Lieutenant Harry ALLEN

28 January 1919
Lieutenant-General Sir Jacobus L. van Deventer KCB, CMG
Commanding-in-Chief, East African Force: General Headquarters, 30th September 1918.
"I desire to record my appreciation of the excellent services rendered by the Officers, Warrant Officers, Non-commissioned Officers and Men included in the list I am forwarding with this Despatch, during the period from 1st December 1917 to 31st July 1918."
Captain Charles GREY MC
Sergeant William D. HARVEY

03 June 1919
Lieutenant-General Sir Jacobus L. van Deventer KCB, CMG
Commanding-in-Chief, East African Force:
"I have the honour to forward herewith my recommendations in favour of the under-mentioned Officers, Ladies, Warrant Officers, Non-commissioned Officers and Men for valuable services rendered during the period 1st August, 1918, to the conclusion of hostilities."
Temporary Lieutenant-Colonel Clive Lancaster CARBUTT

Regimental Sergeant-Major James F. DOUGLAS
Company Sergeant-Major James H. FAURE
Temporary Captain Charles GREY MC
Sergeant LONGWE
Sergeant MAMADI
Sergeant MAYEGA
Sergeant NYONYO
Temporary Captain Henry Thomas ONYETT MC

5 June 1919
Sergeant DANGWE
Private NYAMADI

11 June 1920
"The names of the undermentioned Officers are to be added to those brought to notice for valuable and distinguished services by Lieutenant-General Sir J. L. van Deventer, KCB, CMG, Commanding-in-Chief, East African Force, in his despatch of the 20th January, 1919. (Published in the Supplement of the London Gazette, dated 5th June, 1919)"
Major George James THORNTON OBE

Allied Powers Awards
04 September 1917
War Office, 31 August 1917
"The following are among the Decorations and Medals awarded by the Allied Powers at various dates to the British Forces for distinguished services rendered during the course of the campaign: His Majesty the King has given unrestricted permission in all cases to wear the Decorations and Medals in question."

Silver Medal for Valour (Italy)
For deeds of outstanding gallantry in war
Captain Francis John WANE

Croix de Guerre **(France)**
For individuals who distinguish themselves by acts of heroism involving combat with enemy forces
Lieutenant William James BAKER
Major Clive Lancaster CARBUTT
Second Lieutenant William John CARR
Captain Alexander William FORRESTER (Medical Officer)
Lieutenant William Frederick Croei MORGANS

Medaille Militaire **(France)**
For valour in combat or long service
Sergeant Noel ARNOTT
Sergeant Frederick Edward SIMS
Sergeant Lawrence Charles SYMONS

Appendix III

Honours and Awards RAR and Independent Companies
1st Battalion Rhodesian African Rifles
Pre-UDI

Officer of the Order of the British Empire (OBE)

For services to the Empire

01 June 1953

"The QUEEN has been graciously pleased, on the occasion of Her Majesty's Coronation, to give orders for the following promotions in, and appointments to, the Most Excellent Order of the British Empire: To be Additional Officers of the Military Division of the said Most Excellent Order:"

Lieutenant-Colonel George Edward Litchfield RULE

Rhodesian African Rifles, Southern Rhodesia Military Forces

01 January 1955

"The QUEEN has been graciously pleased to give orders for the following appointments to the Most Excellent Order of the British Empire: To be an Ordinary Officer of the Military Division of the said Most Excellent Order:"

Lieutenant-Colonel George Holland HARTLEY

Rhodesian African Rifles

20 December 1957

"The QUEEN has been graciously pleased to give orders, as on the 30th August, 1957, for the following appointments to the Most Excellent Order of the British Empire, in recognition of distinguished service in Malaya, during the period ending on that date: To be Additional Officers of the Military Division of the said Most Excellent Order:"

Lieutenant-Colonel John ANDERSON

Recommendation citation as endorsed by General Charles Keightley, Commander-in-Chief Far East Land Forces:

"During the year that the 1st Bn The Rhodesian African Rifles have been in Malaya Lt-Col ANDERSON has commanded his Battalion with outstanding ability. The Battalion came inexperienced to operations against Communist Terrorists but very soon the Battalion showed the results of careful training and spirited direction by the Commanding Officer.

Because of their flair for tracking and silent movement the Battalion had been to a great extent employed in the deep jungle where their natural ability has been made full use of. Whilst the Communist Terrorists avoid security forces it becomes increasingly difficult to gain many successes against them in the deep jungle.

Intensive patrolling carried out for long periods without any contact with the Communist Terrorists has been maintained relentlessly. Lacking contacts to sharpen their keenness and efficiency it might be expected that frustration would tend to cause morale to drop in the Battalion. This has been very far from the case. Inspired by Lt-Col ANDERSON's confidence in his men to prove their worth in action against the enemy and with his enthusiasm and rive, morale has risen steadily.

Eventually after much patient work in the deep jungle excellent successes were gained which displayed the Battalion's great dash and eagerness to close with the enemy.

The Commanding Officer himself has taken part in many reconnaissances in the search for Communist Terrorists. Imbued with the determination to eliminate the enemy the Battalion has followed his lead magnificently. When the situation at last allowed the Battalion to operate in the area they know best they have had two recent and highly successful actions. Great courage, determination and outstanding skill in minor tactics and field craft were shown. Morale in the Battalion could not be higher. The keenness and enthusiasm of all ranks is exhilarating. Lt-Col ANDERSON has proved himself an outstanding and courageous Commander whose personality is truly reflected in his Battalion. He is the ideal Commander of the 1st Bn The Rhodesian African Rifles and the leadership he has given has firmly established their reputation as a most successful operational Battalion in Malaya."

12 June 1965

Lieutenant-Colonel William Arthur GODWIN

Imperial Service Order (ISO)

For long and faithful service

06 June 1941

"The KING has been graciously pleased, on the occasion of the Celebration of His Majesty's Birthday, to make the following appointments to the Imperial Service Order: To be Companions of the Order:"

"For services as a Native Commissioner in Southern Rhodesia."

Now Temporary Lieutenant-Colonel Francis John WANE

Member of the Order of the British Empire (MBE)

For services to the Empire

06 June 1946

Major William Hampden Dawson WALKER

Recommendation citation as contained in War Office document 373/82, and endorsed by Lt-General Miles Dempsey, Commander-in-Chief of Allied Land Forces in South East Asia:

"Major WALKER was appointed Adjt of 1RAR when the Regiment was raised in Jul 1940. In July 1942 he was appointed 2IC of the Bn, which position he has held since, except for a brief period when he had temporary command. During this service with the 1RAR he has been largely responsible for the raising, organising and training of the new Battalion. Throughout operations in the ARAKAN up to his going on leave in June 1945, he has proved himself to be an outstanding 2IC. By his personal zeal, extending beyond the duties of his office, he attained a standard of administration throughout the unit, which ensured its success in subsequent operations in the PEGU YOMAS. When placed in control of any operational situation, his outstanding devotion to duty, at times under the most difficult conditions, was an example and inspiration to all ranks which is deserving of recognition."

01 January 1955

Captain Walter Frederick Smith BELTON

23 May 1958

"The QUEEN has been graciously pleased to give orders for the following promotions in, and appointments to, the Most Excellent Order of the British Empire, in recognition of distinguished service in Malaya for the period 31st August to 31st December, 1957: To be Additional Members of the Military Division of the said Most Excellent Order:"

Major Christopher Bernard McCULLAGH

Recommendation citation as endorsed by General Sir Francis Festing, Commander-in-Chief, Far East Land Forces:

"*Since April 1956 Major McCULLAGH has displayed a standard of devotion to duty, personal courage, determination and zeal far in excess of that demanded in the normal course of duty. His skill in operations coupled with his boundless energy and determination to seek out and kill the enemy have been a byword throughout the Battalion. This officer's personal contribution to the Unit's effort against the enemy has been outstanding, and without question has been a most significant factor in achieving the successes so arduously secured. His personal leadership and constant concern and endeavours on behalf of his men has been most marked throughout his long period in the jungle. He has set an example of devotion to duty of the highest order and has richly earned the superb reputation he now enjoys within the unit as a company commander of outstanding merit. He has been recently appointed Second-in-Command of the Battalion. His zeal, his cheerful unbounded enthusiasm together with his flare [sic] for sound administration has been thrown whole-heartedly into his new job. The extremely high standard of maintenance and morale within the regiment is very largely due to Major McCullagh's unfailing devotion to unselfish duty. This officer's service in Malaya has been of such a high quality that it richly deserves recognition of a very high order.*"

Military Cross (MC)

For gallantry during active operations against the enemy awarded, at the time, to captains, lieutenants and warrant officers of the army
20 September 1945
War Service Lieutenant George Victor PITT
(Attached Long Range Desert Group)
Citation: "*In March 1945, Lieutenant Pitt was landed with a small patrol of L.R.D.G. On the Island of Rab (Croatia), where he remained for six weeks. During all this period he was sending back information of enemy movements and positions, which was invaluable to the R.A.F. He carried out many daring and personal reconnaissances [sic] of enemy gun positions and the excellence of his reports enabled the R.A.F. to destroy the majority of them. He was frequently chased by enemy patrols, who knew of his presence, but by continuous movement he was able to avoid capture. When the Partisans landed on Rab Lieutenant Pitt went with them and successfully guided the attacking force on their targets. He later did the same task for the Partisans landing on Cherso and his accurate and quick information was of the utmost value to the R.A.F. Throughout all these and other operations Lieutenant Pitt has shown the greatest courage and enthusiasm and the result of his work has been quite outstanding.*"

Military Medal (MM)

Awarded to NCOs and men of the army for individual or associated acts of bravery
27 August 1957
Platoon Warrant Officer Pisayi MUZERECHO
Recommendation citation as endorsed by General Charles Keightley, Commander-in-Chief Far East Land Forces:
"*On the 8th June 1957 Platoon Warrant Officer PISAYI was commanding his platoon on patrol in the Bekok area of Johore, Malaya. After one of the sections had contacted five armed Communist Terrorists, one of whom was killed, Sergeant Major Pisayi led three other members of the Platoon Headquarters towards the scene of the action and saw the enemy crossing his front. Having been informed of the importance of capturing a Communist Terrorist in this area, Sergeant Major Pisayi chased and captured first one terrorist whom he handed over to another member of his patrol and then chased and captured another. During this time he was repeatedly under fire at short range from two terrorists who had automatic weapons, and also from the men whom he actually captured. The second terrorist*

being captured only after he had expended the ammunition in his pistol, but even he was still armed with a grenade. The capture of these Communist Terrorists by this courageous Warrant Officer is of extreme importance to future operations against the enemy in the area."

20 December 1957
Platoon Warrant Officer Alexander KHUMALO
Recommendation citation as endorsed by General Charles Keightley, Commander-in-Chief Far East Land Forces:
"*Platoon Warrant Officer ALEXANDER was leading a patrol in the Labis District of Johore on the 19th of June 1957. At 6pm his leading scout saw some smoke rising from the jungle edge about four hundred yards north of their position. Realising that the ground to be covered offered very little concealment, Platoon Warrant Officer Alexander ordered his patrol to crawl through the long grass, a distance of two hundred and fifty yards, to a stream where they waited until nightfall. He could then see a fire burning about fifty yards into the jungle – and saw three armed Communist Terrorists standing around the fire. Again he waited, as the noticed the approach of a heavy storm. When it was raining heavily, Platoon Warrant Officer Alexander, with one other soldier, then began to stalk the terrorists. With one of the most daring and skilful acts of fieldcraft imaginable, he crawled towards them. During his approach he had to crawl over the branches of a fallen tree and was often not in position to use his weapon, had he been seen by the enemy. With complete disregard for his personal safety he managed to get within five yards of the terrorists and, signalling to his companion, they fired at the two who were holding their weapons, killing them instantly. The third terrorist, who was wounded, crawled away in the dark and although he twice fired at Platoon Warrant Officer Alexander, he crawled after him and again managed to wound him. In the morning the third terrorist was found and killed. This Warrant officer's leadership, resourcefulness, skill and personal courage, were entirkley responsible for the success of this action and his disregard for personal safety has been an inspiration to the rest of the Battalion.*"

Corporal LENGU
Recommendation citation as endorsed by General Charles Keightley, Commander-in-Chief Far East Land Forces:
"*Corporal LENGU has shown exceptional keenness, efficiency and offensive spirit in operations against the Communist Terrorists in the period covered by this report (January to May 1957). He has always proved himself to be a courageous and resourceful NCO, always willing to undertake the most hazardous of operations. On the 16th May 1957, in the Segamat District of Johore, Corporal Lengu was in charge of a patrol. His leading scout stopped, indicating that he had heard voices ahead. Corporal Lengu ordered the patrol to halt whilst he went forward to reconnoitre. He crept forward silently until he came to a small clearing where he saw four armed Communist Terrorists. These terrorists were obviously suspicious and on the alert with their weapons at the ready. Realising that there was no time to call up the rest of the patrol, and make an organised assault, Corporal Lengu decided to attack them himself. To make his attack he would have to cross the clearing in full view of the terrorists at a range of about ten yards. With complete disregard for his own safety and fully realising that he could expect no help from the members of his patrol who were some distance behind, Corporal Lengu charged straight at the Communist Terrorists. As soon as they heard the sound of his assault two of the terrorists took cover at the jungle edge to cover the retreat of the remaining two who turned to engage Corporal Lengu with rifle fire. The suddenness and speed of Corporal Lengu's assault so disrupted the terrorists that they were unable to return his fire and he killed the two in the clearing. The two remaining terrorists, seeing the deaths of their comrades, turned and ran, pursued by Corporal Lengu. He followed them for some distance, but lost their tracks and was forced to return to the clearing where he collected the rest of his patrol. This extremely brave, gallant and single-handed action by Corporal Lengu against*

four armed Communist Terrorists is an example of personal bravery which has inspired the rest of the Battalion.”

The British Empire Medal (BEM)

For meritorious military service awarded to ranks below warrant officer

11 June 1960

“The QUEEN has been graciously pleased, on the occasion of the Celebration of Her Majesty's Birthday, and on the advice of Her Majesty's Ministers of the Federation of Rhodesia and Nyasaland, to approve the award of the British Empire Medal (Military Division) to the undermentioned:”

Warrant Officer Class II CHIWAYA

02 June 1962

“The QUEEN has been graciously pleased, on the occasion of the Celebration of Her Majesty's Birthday, and on the advice of Her Majesty's Ministers of the Federation of Rhodesia and Nyasaland, to approve the award of the British Empire Medal (Military Division) to the undermentioned:”

Warrant Officer Class II MATAMBO
Rhodesia and Nyasaland Army

13 June 1964

“The QUEEN has been graciously pleased, on the occasion of the Celebration of Her Majesty's Birthday, to approve the award of the British Empire Medal (Military Division) to the undermentioned:”

Warrant Officer Class II Jairos MUTEPFA

01 January 1965

“The QUEEN has been graciously pleased to approve the award of the British Empire Medal (Military Division) to the undermentioned:”

Colour-Sergeant TADERERA
Warrant Officer Class I S. MURUDU

Mentioned in Despatches

Commanders in the field submitted periodical reports to the commander-in-chief, which were known as dispatches. These would sometimes contain names of officers and men whose actions significantly contributed to the campaign, for the commanding general's consideration. Those 'mentioned in dispatches' after 1914 were awarded with oak leaf insignia to be attached to the campaign medal ribbon.

30 December 1941

“The KING has been graciously pleased to approve that the following be Mentioned in recognition of distinguished services in the Middle East (including Egypt, East Africa, The Western Desert, The Sudan, Greece, Crete, Syria and Tobruk) during the period February, 1941, to July, 1941:”

Sergeant O.H. TEMPLAR

01 November 1945

Temporary Major Stanley Ernest MORRIS
Initially recommended for the Military Cross
Citation: *“During the attack on a strongly defended enemy position on the Tanlwe Chaung, ARAKAN on 26*

April 1945 the leading platoon of Major Morris' company were engaged by heavy LMG and MMG fire and his only remaining Subaltern Officer was wounded. The Company hesitated to go forward and the Company losing its momentum, Major Morris immediately came forward and with complete disregard for his own safety personally encouraged his men forward along the narrow precipitous track which was the only approach to the enemy machine gun position. By his own personal example and determination Major Morris restored the situation and led his men into the enemy position where they silenced the machine gun and took the objective despite casualties.”

19 September 1946

“The KING has been graciously pleased to approve that the following be Mentioned in recognition of gallant and distinguished services in Burma.”

Sergeant BENJAMIN
Sergeant CHAMUNORWA
Temporary Major C.S. DAVIES
Company Sergeant-Major ELIJAH
Company Sergeant-Major T.M. FERREIRA
Acting Major G.H. HARTLEY
Staff Sergeant M.W. HESKETH
Temporary R.W. LOWINGS
Temporary Captain A.S. VALENTINE
Lieutenant V.V. MANNIX
Lieutenant O.H. TEMPLAR
Captain R.B. WALKER

23 May 1958

“The QUEEN has been graciously pleased to approve that the following names be mentioned in recognition of gallant and distinguished services in Malaya for the period 31st August to 31st December, 1957:”

Captain William T.D. de HAAST
Major F.S. FITZGERALD
Temporary Major William A. GODWIN
Lieutenant F.G.David HEPPENSTALL
Major John S. SALT
Captain John Ryan SHAW
Lieutenant John R. WELLS-WEST

Certificate of Gallantry

Sgt Phillip
Pte Mirimi

Special Commendation in Force Orders (Southern Rhodesia)

Lt G.H. Barlow
Lt J.R. Inskipp

Commander in Chief's Commendation

Pte Nyikavaranda

1st Battalion Rhodesian African Rifles
Post-UDI

Silver Cross of Rhodesia (SCR)
For conspicuous gallantry
08 September 1978
Lance Corporal Chamunorwa SARIROWONA

Citation: *"Since February 1976 L/Cpl Sarirowona of B Company 1RAR has been involved in a number of contacts with terrorists. At all times he has displayed outstanding determination to close with and eliminate terrorists, first as a private soldier and since 1977, as a lance-corporal. He has led by example throughout this period, inspiring those around him with gallant and aggressive acts in the face of the enemy. On 2 April, he was one of a small group of soldiers undergoing specialized training at a base camp in the operational area. The sub-unit normally resident at this base camp was out on duty. The soldiers were all volunteers under training for special tasks, and in addition, they protected the camp. At approximately 2100 hours the sentry reported possible terrorist movement to the south of the camp. While occupants of the base camp were in the process of moving to stand-to positions, approximately twenty terrorists opened fire on them with mortars and small arms. All the soldiers took cover immediately except for the platoon commander and L Cpl Sarirowona who ran to firing positions close to and overlooking the terrorist position. Armed only with a sub-machine gun and one full magazine of ammunition, L Cpl Sarirowona closed to within 100 metres of the terrorists. With complete disregard for his own safety he continually exposed himself to enemy fire under very hazardous circumstances in an attempt to direct aimed bursts of fire at the enemy. In this position a terrorist mortar bomb exploded approximately 20 metres behind him and he was wounded in the shoulder and leg with shrapnel. The wounds did not stop him from continuing to return fire at the terrorists until he had expended all his ammunition. Throughout the action he shouted abuse at the terrorists and challenged them to come closer. Finally deterred by the fierce reaction of the base camp occupants, the terrorists took flight. Despite his wounds, L Cpl Sarirowona assisted his officer in re-organising the other soldiers and re-issued ammunition before he sought medical attention. As soon as possible after recovery from these wounds, he returned to the operational area. On 27 June 1977, along with other members of his platoon, he was a passenger in a vehicle in the operational area. At approximately 1600 hours the vehicle came under effective fire from an estimated group of forty terrorists who were in a well-sited ambush position. The initial enemy fire wounded nine of the eleven passengers in the vehicle, and having sustained mechanical damage from the terrorist fire, the vehicle came to a halt well within effective range of the terrorists' weapons. L Cpl Sarirowona was one of the two passengers who escaped injury, and seeing the plight of his wounded comrades attempting to take cover, he took the only machine gun from a wounded man and proceeded to provide effective covering fire for his comrades. He did so from a completely exposed position and kept up his covering fire while the other uninjured passenger assisted the wounded off the vehicle and into cover. Despite their numerical superiority and their superior fire power, the terrorists soon abandoned their efforts and withdrew, which must be attributed to L Cpl Sarirowona's courageous display of aggressiveness. Since this incident, L Cpl Sarirowona has been engaged in further contacts and wounded again with a gunshot in the leg on 13 January 1978, since when he has made a strenuous effort to become fit enough to return to operations. These examples of this NCO's gallantry and leadership coupled with his complete contempt for the enemy and his aggressive determination to eliminate them have been, and continue to be, an example and inspiration to his fellow soldiers."*

30 June 1980
Lieutenant Patrick LAWLESS

Citation: *"Lieutenant Patrick Lawless joined the 1st Battalion, the Rhodesian African Rifles on 4 February 1977 as a platoon commander. Throughout his service he has displayed a fierce determination to seek out and destroy the enemy. He has frequently been exposed to extremely dangerous situations in which his calm planning and aggressive action have been outstanding. On 11 August 1978, Lt Lawless was in command of a group of seven men tasked with locating a route which was being used by terrorists to infiltrate Rhodesia. Towards last light Lt Lawless' group located a group of three terrorists moving through the area. By skilful and prompt manoeuvre of his men, he succeeded in wounding and capturing one of these terrorists although darkness had fallen by the time contact was made. The terrorist died of his wounds in spite of Lt Lawless' efforts to keep him alive, but before dying, he yielded valuable information. The following morning, a group of terrorists, numbering approximately seventy, carried out a surprise attack on Lt Lawless' group. The terrorists, who enjoyed tactical and numerical superiority, made repeated fierce and determined attacks on the small patrol. Lt Lawless so organized and inspired his men that the terrorists were driven back each time until, desperately short of ammunition; he was forced to conduct a tactical withdrawal. At least eight terrorists were killed and a number of others wounded in this action. On another occasion Lt Lawless was a member of a Fireforce which responded to a sighting of thirty terrorists. Following a series of contacts with this group, Lt Lawless was tasked to command a sweep to clear the river line along which the terrorists had taken cover. The sweep line was subjected to heavy small-arms and machine-gun fire. Lt Lawless was ordered by the Fireforce commander to withdraw to facilitate use of air weapons against the terrorists' position. During the regrouping phase, Lt Lawless realized that one officer was missing. Siting machine guns to cover his movement and undaunted by the heavy enemy fire being directed at him, Lt Lawless skirmished alone to the last reported position of the missing officer. He located the officer who had been mortally wounded approximately eight metres from the terrorists' position. The close proximity to the enemy position prohibited the use of air weapons against the terrorists, so Lt Lawless rapidly assessed the situation and moved his machine gun to a better position. In this assault, three terrorists were killed. The sweep line then continued with its task, successfully eliminating a further seven terrorists in the process. On reaching a sharp river bend, the sweep came under heavy and effective fire from six terrorists who had positioned themselves among boulders in the riverbed. Lt Lawless moved his men to a position from which they could provide effective covering fire for an assault group on the other side of the river. The initial assault was successful but resulted in one of the officers being wounded in the head. Lt Lawless, appreciating the demoralising effect that the wounded officer would have on his men unless he was attended to rapidly, moved to his assistance. This entailed crossing a river in full view of the terrorists and under heavy small-arms fire. With complete disregard for his own safety, Lt Lawless successfully reached the wounded officer, rendered first aid, and arranged the necessary casevac. He then resumed command of the sweep line and so manoeuvred his men as to facilitate the elimination by the sweep of a further three terrorists. In this fierce action fifteen terrorists in all were accounted for, and a great deal of credit for the success achieved must go to Lt Lawless whose calm leadership and fearless actions inspired those about him. In the aforementioned actions and numerous others in which Lt Lawless has been involved, he has repeatedly committed acts of conspicuous gallantry in his determination to close with the enemy. He has earned the undying respect and admiration of those with whom he serves and his conduct is worthy of the highest praise and recognition."*

Officer of the Order of the Legion of Merit (OLM)
For distinguished service to Rhodesia
11 November 1978
Brigadier Herbert BARNARD, DCD

13 April 1979
Brigadier Michael Douglas SHUTE
For distinguished service in the Rhodesian Army

Member of the Order of the Legion of Merit (MLM)

For distinguished service to Rhodesia

12 July 1971

Major Frederick George David HEPPENSTALL

Citation: *"Major F.G.D. Heppenstall was posted to the 1st Battalion, the Rhodesian African Rifles as a company commander on 10 December 1963, and he is still serving with this unit in this capacity. The company commanded by this officer had achieved outstanding success in counter-insurgency operations. The company has spent many long and arduous periods on operations yet the morale, efficiency and determination of the men remains at peak level. This high standard can only be attributed to the outstanding leadership qualities and high sense of duty of Major F.G.D Heppenstall. His example and determination is an inspiring example to all who may be associated with him."*

26 September 1975

Major Peter James BURFORD

Citation: *"For distinguished service in a combatant role in the northeast border area. Major Burford served with the 1st Battalion, the Rhodesian African Rifles as a company commander for several years. On his posting to the regiment he was almost immediately deployed with his men on operations. He soon revealed his outstanding ability as a field commander. On several occasions he led his men on foot into inaccessible regions of the Zambezi Valley, where water was scarce and re-supply impossible. At all times his personal example was an inspiration to his men. His determination and his aggressive spirit contributed immeasurably to the success of the company's operations. In the latter months of his service with the Battalion, Major Burford was twice appointed field commander of a high-density force, consisting of several companies. On both occasions the operations were eminently successful in that they resulted in the elimination of a total of nineteen terrorists, of whom three were notorious gang leaders. His detailed planning and preparation, and swift execution were, in no small way, contributing factors to the success of these units under his command. Major Burford never ceased in his search for new methods of combating terrorists. He continually strove for perfection in the training and operational techniques of his company. His devotion to duty and exemplary conduct in the field and in barracks have been an inspiration to those who have served with him."*

15 October 1976

Warrant Officer Class II Chiyanike MUZONDIDA

Citation: *"In the past three years, Warrant Officer Muzondida has been engaged in continuous anti-terrorist duties. In these actions Warrant Officer Muzondida has displayed outstanding aggression and courage, contributing in no small way to the successes achieved. In recent years he has frequently been required to command a platoon for extended periods, both in barracks and on operations. His diligence and leadership have been of the highest order and have resulted in his platoon attaining a high standard of morale and efficiency. In many operations Warrant Officer Muzondida has had European soldiers placed under his command. His personality, common sense and high standard of professionalism have enabled him not only to overcome many difficulties of command but also to engender mutual confidence and respect to a marked degree. His quality as a leader and a platoon commander may best be measured by the high morale of his men and their successes in battle. In addition to being an outstanding combat leader, Warrant Officer Muzondida has more recently demonstrated his versatility by excelling as a liaison officer between his company and tribesmen living in the operational area. His sound advice, excellent knowledge of human behaviour, and management capabilities engendered an unprecedented spirit of co-operation and trust between tribesmen and security forces, thus contributing immeasurably to the success of a complex civil/military venture. Warrant Officer Muzondida displayed an ability and devotion to duty consistently, and of the highest order. His leadership, courage, initiative and unswerving allegiance have been a constant example and inspiration to all those who have served with and alongside him."*

23 September 1977

Major Bernard SCHLACHTER

Citation: *"For distinguished service in a combatant role and exceptional professional attributes as a company commander. Major Schlachter has served with the 1st Battalion, the Rhodesian African Rifles, in a combatant role, continually for four years. On 1 April 1976, he was tasked with forming Support Company of the battalion with a nucleus of officers, warrant officers, non-commissioned officers and a great number of recruits. By example, hard work and determination this company was welded into an outstanding sub-unit. Only six weeks after formation, the .Support Company was deployed on operations in May 1976 and under the personal leadership of Major Schlachter were responsible for the elimination of twenty-eight terrorists in a three week period while on Fireforce. In the last year Major Schlachter has shown outstanding ability as a field commander. He has commanded large combined army, air force and police actions most commendably and with great success. Major Schlachter, over the extended period he has been employed in the combatant role, never ceases in his search for new methods of combating terrorists. He continually strives for perfection in the formation, training and operational techniques of his company. His devotion to duty, exemplary and professional conduct in the field and barracks are an inspiring example to all."*

11 November 1977

Major David S. DRAKE

Lieutenant N. Martin TUMBARE DMM

Bronze Cross of Rhodesia (BCR)

For gallantry

23 October 1970

Second Lieutenant Ronald MARILLIER

Citation: *"For gallantry and leadership in action. 2nd Lt Marillier, a newly commissioned officer, in command of inexperienced troops, was ordered to withdraw from an exposed position where he and his men had become pinned down under heavy enemy fire. With complete disregard for his own safety, 2nd Lt Marillier crawled over exposed ground, under heavy enemy fire and succeeded in redeploying his men. Throughout this difficult action, 2nd Lt Marillier displayed great gallantry for so young and inexperienced an officer and his conduct was an inspiration to all those present at the action."*

Platoon Warrant Officer Wurayayi MUTERO

Citation: *"For gallantry and leadership in action. Sergeant Major Wurayayi Mutero has taken part in numerous anti-terrorist operations and has been involved in a number of contacts with the enemy. His performance on all these occasions has been outstanding and his determination, qualities of leadership and complete disregard for his own safety have been an inspiration to the men he commands."*

Private Kenias TOVAKARE

Citation: *"For gallantry and devotion to duty in action. As a radio operator in a fierce engagement against terrorists, Pte Tovakare remained with his commander and maintained his duties under extremely hazardous conditions until, because of the danger; his commander took over the radio set from him. Later, when as a result of being severely wounded, his commander was forced to abandon the radio, Pte Tovakare, realizing that communications were essential, retrieved the radio and two weapons at great personal risk. Throughout the engagement Pte Tovakare displayed gallantry and devotion to duty under extremely dangerous conditions."*

Lieutenant Ian Patrick WARDLE

"For gallantry and leadership in action. During anti-terrorist operations, while leading a patrol in pursuit of a gang of terrorists, Lt Wardle and his men found themselves in the centre of a well-concealed terrorist position. Lt Wardle immediately directed a heavy weight of fire at one terrorist position thus killing two terrorists and causing the surrender of a further four. On learning from one surrendered terrorist that other terrorists were concealed nearby, Lt Wardle, with complete disregard for his own safety, immediately positioned himself where he could subject this area to fire and, in the ensuing battle, a further six terrorists were killed and two captured. The success of this action can only be attributed to Lt Wardle's quick, fearless action and remarkable qualities of leadership."

13 September 1974
Private Phinias FOSHORE

Citation: "For gallantry and determination in action. During anti-terrorist operations in the north eastern border area, the platoon of which Pte Phinias was a member was engaged in a contact with twelve to fourteen terrorists. During the engagement Pte Phinias was shot at point blank range through the upper arm by a terrorist. Realising that he could not handle his weapon, he dropped his rifle and attacked the terrorist with his hands, forcing him to the ground before another shot could be fired. During the struggle, while he was attempting to overcome the terrorist with his bare hands, Pte Phinias was again shot in the back by another terrorist. In spite of his wounds, Pte Phinias continued to grapple with the terrorist, refusing to let go until the terrorist was shot and killed and he was assisted off the body. Pte Phinias, who had only recently completed his recruit training, displayed outstanding determination, courage and aggressive spirit for such a young and inexperienced soldier."

Warrant Officer 2nd Class Gibson MUGADZA

Citation: "For gallantry and leadership. While serving as a platoon warrant officer in anti-terrorist operations in the north-eastern border area, Warrant Officer Gibson Mugadza has been involved in numerous engagements with the terrorists, in which he has displayed outstanding qualities of courage, determination and leadership. In an encounter while occupying a night ambush position and seeing three terrorists he could not effectively engage with fire, he took three of his men and followed up until he was within close range when he engaged with and killed them. In another engagement he was in a stop-line position at night with four men when they were attacked from the rear by approximately ten terrorists who put down heavy fire on his position, killing one soldier. With his machine gun out of action and only three weapons firing, Warrant Officer Gibson Mugadza stood his ground and in spite of being outnumbered and facing greatly superior fire power, repulsed the attack. Warrant Officer Gibson Mugadza moved to a better position, first removing all equipment from the dead soldier so that it could not fall into enemy hands. Having re-organized his defences and encouraging the other three soldiers, his own bravery and determined leadership enabled the small group to beat off three more vigorous attacks during the night. His personal courage and outstanding qualities of leadership under conditions of extreme danger were an inspiration to his men and prevented his position from being overrun."

26 September 1975
Sergeant Abedenice Ntulini MAZINGANE

Citation: "For continuous gallantry and leadership in action. Sergeant Ntulini has been involved in ten contacts with terrorists over the past two and a half years. In these contacts Sergeant Ntulini showed a great degree of reliability as a leader, particularly under fire. In Sergeant Ntulini his men recognized a man of infinite patience and a sense of purpose. In one contact Sergeant Ntulini was involved with six terrorists. He assisted in killing five of the enemy and was an inspiration to the limited number of troops involved in the contact; he made it his business to be in the thick of the fighting and appeared to lack fear by constantly supporting and encouraging the men around him. On another occasion three terrorists were sighted and eight men, commanded by Sergeant Ntulini were despatched to the area. The contact that ensued was a text-book encounter involving excellent use of ground and weapons. The use of grenades was superb and devastating, and the ruthless extermination of the gang was entirely attributable to Sergeant Ntulini's common sense, quick action and bold approach. The senior member of this gang was later identified as a sectorial political commissar who had been in the area for 18 months. His death had far-reaching results.

On a more recent occasion while Sergeant Ntulini was a stick commander, twenty-four well-armed terrorists had laid an ambush on high ground around a re-entrant for the platoon that was following their tracks. As the platoon approached, Ntulini heard talking and immediately informed his platoon commander. Having done this, he moved back to his stick which was on high ground on one side of the re-entrant. The platoon came under very heavy fire. However, thanks to his alertness, Sergeant Ntulini prevented the platoon from being surprised. The firefight continued until the platoon skirmished forward and succeeded in clearing the terrorists from the high ground. The terrorist leader, with two other terrorists, saw the assault group and decided to slip into the re-entrant. This move was spotted by Sergeant Ntulini who moved his men to a favourable position and they then killed all three terrorists. One, if not two, of the terrorists was shot by Sergeant Ntulini himself. It was undoubtedly due to the courage, initiative, professional skill and good leadership of Sergeant Ntulini that what could have been a disastrous situation was turned into a successful contact, resulting in three enemy killed, one of whom was a terrorist leader. Successes in these and other engagements were entirely attributable to the outstanding powers of leadership, enthusiasm and determined aggression in action by Sergeant Ntulini which have been a constant inspiration to all."

15 October 1976
Warrant Officer 2nd Class Moses PONGWENI

Citation: "Warrant Officer Pongweni has, for the past 18 months, been engaged in continuous anti-terrorist operations, both as a platoon warrant officer and, in recent months, as a platoon commander. During this period his platoon has been involved in numerous contacts with terrorists in which several of the enemy have been killed and captured. In all these engagements Warrant Officer Pongweni displayed outstanding aggression and leadership. On one occasion Warrant Officer Pongweni and his platoon were flown into stop positions ahead of a follow-up group. When it became apparent that the terrorists had slipped through the net, Warrant Officer Pongweni and his stick were flown into a contact while the battle was in progress. Under fire from the time they de-planed, Warrant Officer Pongweni demonstrated his leadership and calmness by deploying his men into an excellent cut-off position, thus sealing the fate of the terrorist group. In this contact all seven members of the terrorist group were eliminated and this success was due in no small measure to Warrant Officer Pongweni's courage and determination. On another occasion, Warrant Officer Pongweni and his patrol of six men were operating in a remote area of the Honde Valley. Shortly before last light the patrol was ambushed by 15 to 20 terrorists in well-prepared positions. In the first few seconds of the contact one member of the patrol was killed and another injured. Warrant Officer Pongweni himself was in a totally exposed position but with complete disregard for his own safety and under heavy fire at close range, he immediately engaged the terrorists. Such was his example that he was joined by his machine gunner and together they put the terrorists to flight. Rallying the survivors, Warrant Officer Pongweni gave chase to the terrorists before returning to tend to his dead and wounded. In this engagement there can be no doubt that Warrant Officer Pongweni's personal courage in the face of heavy fire was instrumental in saving the lives of his patrol in a critical situation. More recently, Warrant Officer Pongweni and his platoon were returning to base by vehicle when they were ambushed by between 15 and 20 terrorists firing from across a broad and deep river. Warrant Officer Pongweni's presence of mind and rapid orders to his driver enabled the leading vehicle to clear the killing area without loss. Realizing that he was unable to cross the river to assault the terrorist position, Warrant Officer

Pongweni skilfully deployed his troops under fire to an excellent position overlooking the area of thick bush in which the terrorists were hiding. Within seconds he had two machine guns in action and very quickly regained the initiative. Such was the effectiveness of the fire that some of the terrorists broke and fled while the remainder, although unseen in the dense bush, were pinned down and remained so until the arrival of Fireforce. Throughout the engagement which lasted for two hours, Warrant Officer Pongweni was in complete control of the situation and his personal leadership and example were an inspiration to all. Warrant Officer Pongweni's initiative as a platoon commander and his courage and leadership in battle has earned him the respect and admiration of his men. His constant good humour in adversity and his unswerving allegiance have been an inspiration to all who have served with him."

29 October 1976
Warrant Officer 2nd Class Yangama KUPARA

Citation: *"Warrant Officer Kupara has been continually involved in counter-insurgency operations since 1967, a total of nine years. During this time he has progressed from section commander to company sergeant-major and has shown outstanding qualities of leadership and competence. Due to the shortage of junior officers, Warrant Officer Kupara frequently commanded platoons on operations for long periods with exceptional ability. In October 1974, he commanded 2 Platoon of A Company 1RAR when they had two very successful contacts, resulting in the death of three terrorist leaders among eight eliminations. On 7 January 1975, Warrant Officer Kupara was leading a patrol which had a fleeting contact with a number of terrorists. He carried out immediate and aggressive action and killed one terrorist personally by a direct hit with a rifle grenade. Since January 1976, A Company has taken part in Fireforce operations at regular intervals and have had notable successes. Several kills and captures were attributable to the courage, calmness, tactical skill and excellent bush craft of Warrant Officer Kupara. On a contact on 3 April 1976, Warrant Officer Kupara and his stick were pinned down by accurate fire by a terrorist using an RPD machine-gun. Warrant Officer Kupara threw a white phosphorus grenade and under its cover, moved around behind the RPD gunner and shot him through the head, killing him. Three other terrorists were also killed in this contact. On the night of 6 May 1976, Warrant Officer Kupara was commanding the lead vehicle of two vehicles carrying 2 Platoon and Company Tactical Headquarters of A Company when the rear vehicle was ambushed by eight to ten terrorists using RPG, RPD and small arms. The vehicle was immobilized and one section commander was killed on the vehicle. Warrant Officer Kupara immediately stopped his vehicle, which was out of the killing zone, and directed rifle-grenade fire on to the terrorist position followed by an immediate clearance of the position. Warrant Officer Kupara showed a calm professional approach and handled his men in an excellent manner throughout. His determination and confidence had an excellent effect, especially upon some of the younger soldiers, recently out of recruit training, who must have been somewhat shaken by the ambush and death of the section commander during darkness. Warrant Officer Kupara has a quiet personality, but is an experienced and well-respected soldier. His tactical ability and calmness in action are first class at all times. He has displayed continuous bravery and competence on counter-insurgency operations over a long period."*

Second Lieutenant Dennis C. PASSAPORTIS

Citation: *"Second Lieutenant Passaportis is a platoon commander in A Company 1RAR. During the period 1 February to 18 May 1976, he deployed on opera with his company. A considerable time was spent on Fireforce duties in which 2nd Lt Passaportis acted as ground force commander on numerous occasions. In all, 2nd Lt Passaportis took part in eight contacts, the majority of which were highly successful, resulting in the elimination of numerous terrorists. On 13 May, 2nd Lt Passaportis was dropped with his stick in an area where about ten terrorists had been contacted. His stick soon came under very accurate and well-controlled fire from a thickly wooded area near a terrorist*

camp, which effectively pinned him down. During an attempt to take the terrorist position he was superficially wounded in the hand and his combat cap was shot off. Despite the fact that two further contacts were taking place nearby, he directed supporting fire to within ten metres of his own position and moved to a more favourable position to attempt a third assault. During this manoeuvre he came under further accurate fire and one of his soldiers was mortally wounded in the chest. 2nd Lt Passaportis crawled forward under fire into the open and dragged the wounded soldier to cover, where he rendered first aid. Throughout the contact which lasted about five hours, repeated air strikes took place and all the aircraft and ground troops were under accurate fire. During this time, 2nd Lt Passaportis gave calm and accurate target indication orders. These were of great assistance to his company commander as Fireforce commander. His calmness and aggression were an inspiration to the troops under his command. On 18 May, the Fireforce was again deployed to a contact during which a terrorist was flushed from cover and wounded. Appreciating the importance of information, the Fireforce commander dropped 2nd Lt Passaportis' stick close by to affect a capture, as the terrorist had dropped his weapon some distance away. When 2nd Lt Passaportis ordered the wounded terrorist to stand up, the terrorist threw a grenade which he had concealed 2nd Lt Passaportis and another soldier both received serious injuries and the terrorist was killed by the remainder of the stick. Despite the fact that he had sixty-two shrapnel wounds from the grenade, 2nd Lt Passaportis was back in the operational area in less than five weeks after he had been wounded. During all his contacts, 2nd Lt Passaportis has remained cool, calm, cheerful and most efficient. In addition to his obvious bravery, he has shown a keen and subtle sense of humour which has contributed greatly to a high state of morale in his sub-unit. The soldiers under his command have complete confidence in his abilities and he never expects them to do anything which he is not prepared to do himself."

25 March 1977
Acting Corporal James MAKUWA (Posthumous)

Citation: *"Corporal Makuwa was part of Fireforce that responded to a call on 30 April 1976 that an army sub-unit was in contact with about 20 terrorists, three of whom had been killed. During observation duties, Corporal Makuwa, in charge of one position, sighted thirteen terrorists attempting to escape from the contact area. The position of these terrorists was indicated to the pilot and the gunner of the aircraft by Corporal Makuwa, and a second contact ensued, with a firefight developing between the aircraft and the terrorists. Corporal Makuwa's stick was then deployed to take part in the contact and accounted for two terrorists killed. In the ensuing action a further four terrorists were killed. His stick was then instructed to regroup and while moving towards the rendezvous they came under heavy fire from two terrorists. Fire was immediately returned and the terrorists were wounded and surrendered. The success achieved in this action can be attributed to a large degree to Corporal Makuwa's initiative, personal courage and qualities of leadership. It was as a result of this and many previous successful actions that Corporal Makuwa had been recommended for promotion to sergeant but, regrettably, this fine non-commissioned officer died as a result of wounds received after a follow-up on 9 May 1976."*

29 July 1977
Lance Corporal M. MAGARA

13 October 1978
Warrant Officer 2nd Class Abias MASHONA

Citation: *"Warrant Officer 2nd Class Mashona has been continually involved in counter-insurgency operations since 1967. During this time, he has progressed from private to warrant officer class II and has shown outstanding qualities of leadership, courage and professionalism. As a junior soldier he was involved in numerous engagements during which his aggression and courage contributed greatly to the elimination of the enemy. Such were his qualities that he was periodically drafted to Special Forces for specific operations. Warrant Officer 2nd Class Mashona has studied the enemy in detail. Utilising this knowledge he has shown an exceptional ability to locate enemy groups and on one occasion, armed with only a pistol, and with complete disregard for his own safety, Warrant Officer 2nd Class Mashona entered an area known to be occupied by terrorists. Exercising guile and cunning, he located the enemy group and then guided ground- and air-borne forces on to their positions. Eight of the enemy was killed and two were captured, together with important documents and quantities of weapons and equipment. On two other occasions similar successes were recorded as a result of his perseverance to remain undetected in hostile areas for protracted periods. On all the above occasions, Warrant Officer 2nd Class Mashona received high praise from ground- and air-borne commanders for his accuracy and the simple and clear-cut manner in which he directed them onto the enemy. As a member of the Fireforce, Warrant Officer 2nd Class Mashona has proved to be courageous and aggressive and has recorded a number of personal kills. On two occasions while at home in the Tribal Trust Lands, Warrant Officer 2nd Class Mashona has been sought by the enemy. On one of these occasions, seven terrorists surrounded his house and called for him to surrender. With determined and intelligent actions, he managed to escape. He then gave up his leave, returned to the area in a clandestine manner and was able to locate this enemy group and call in forces to a successful contact. Warrant Officer 2nd Class Mashona has earned the unqualified respect of the officers and men of his unit. His unswerving allegiance, dedication, professional ability and bravery are a constant high example and inspiration to all."*

09 February 1979
Private Ernest RASHAMIRE

Citation: *"Private Rashamire has served with Support Company, 1ˢᵗ Battalion, the Rhodesian African Rifles, since January 1977 during which time he has been involved in numerous contacts with communist terrorists. In all of these actions he has displayed an outstanding determination to eliminate the enemy. On one occasion he was a member of an eight-man section which made contact with a group of approximately seventy terrorists. Several terrorists were killed in the initial firefight, but in an unusual display of tenacity, probably related to their greatly superior numerical strength, the terrorists kept up the attack. Under covering fire from their companions a group of about 20 terrorists attempted to outflank the small army patrol from an area of high and dominating ground. The only member of the Security Force patrol to observe this group's movement was Private Rashamire. Realising the tactical advantage that the terrorists would achieve if they gained the dominating ground, Private Rashamire left his covered position and with complete disregard for his own safety, charged at the group, firing his weapon as he ran. He killed two terrorists outright and successfully changed any persistent intentions on the part of the remainder by throwing a hand grenade into their midst. Private Rashamire's daring act caused the terrorists to flee, thus denying them the use of tactically important ground from which they would almost certainly have inflicted casualties upon the Security Force patrol. His gallantry and clear thinking under the extremely perilous conditions prevailing at the time were an inspiration to those about him and serve as an example to all."*

Defence Force Cross for Distinguished Service (DCD)
For distinguished service
11 November 1975
Colonel Herbert BARNARD

Defence Forces Medal for Meritorious Service (DMM)
For meritorious service
12 July 1971
Warrant Officer Class I N. TUMBARE

11 November 1971
Lieutenant-Colonel W.A. GODWIN OBE

10 July 1972
Warrant Officer Class I E. Campion
Warrant Officer Class II O. VEREMU

11 November 1975
Major K.R. MACDONALD

Citation: *"In 1964 Major (then Lieutenant) Macdonald arrived to take charge of the regimental band of the Rhodesian African Rifles. It is no secret that, at that time, the band's efficiency and ability were only mediocre. In a classic display of single-minded determination and initiative, combined with a high professional ability, Major Macdonald very quickly produced what is acknowledged to be the finest military band in this country. To achieve and maintain this status naturally required a great deal of hard work and long hours. Major Macdonald never faltered or failed to give of his best. By virtue of his post, Major Macdonald became a roving ambassador for the Rhodesian Army and no organization could have wished for a finer such ambassador. His name is now known with affection throughout the country. It is significant that, in an army which prides itself on the high standards for which it is known throughout the military world, Major Macdonald is one of a handful of members who have been decorated with the Defence Forces Medal for Meritorious Service."*

Warrant Officer Class II J. MAHOBOYO
Warrant Officer Class II P. MPINI

11 November 1976
Major B.V. HULLEY
Warrant Officer Class II R. KURIRIRAYI
Warrant Officer Class II D. NYAGUMBO

11 November 1977
Warrant Officer Class I J.C BVUDZI

Citation: *"WOI Bvudzi attested into the army on 7 September 1954 and was posted to 1RAR where he joined D Company as a private soldier. He went to Malaya with the Battalion and while there, went on a four-month cookery course with the British Army Catering Corps Far East Training Centre. He achieved top honours and since then has given outstanding service to his regiment and the army as a cook and caterer. As senior caterer in the regiment, WOI Bvudzi has, among other responsibilities, been solely in charge of the training of all cooks and with the formation of 2RAR and the Depot, he set about the task of training all the new cooks that were required. The results that were achieved from the courses were exceptional, particularly in view of the sometimes indifferent material he had to train. During these courses he has provided, from personal funds, prizes for the best cooks, one of the many examples of his selflessness in the army's interests. An outstanding member of the back-room team, his devotion to his sometimes thankless task and his contribution to the army during his 23 years' service are deserving of high praise and recognition."*

Warrant Officer Class I T.M. CHIDUKU
Citation: *"WOI Chiduku attested into the Rhodesian Army on 10 September 1962 and was posted to 1RAR. In*

June 1965, he was promoted to WOI. During his service he has achieved outstanding success in the schools of which he has been headmaster. By his example of diligence and loyalty to his staff, he has gendered the highest professional standards and results. In his dealings with staff, pupils and parents, he has more than fulfilled his responsibilities as a headmaster and has significantly contributed to the maintenance of morale within the unit and to the esteem in which his school is held."

Warrant Officer Class II J. CHITEREKA
Major C.J. DU PREEZ
Citation: *"Major du Preez has been quartermaster to 1RAR since 1975. During this time the battalion has run both a main and rear headquarters and Major du Preez has proved himself an outstanding quartermaster in his administration of the Headquarters Rear and his provisioning of the battalion in the field. His drive, energy and devotion have ensured that no one has gone without necessary re-supply. This attitude has ensured efficiency within the battalion and the many sub-units under Battalion HQ never cease to praise him for the logistical support they receive."*

11 November 1978
Captain E.I.A. CRACKNELL
RhAPC attached 1RAR
Citation: *"Captain Cracknell served as paymaster to the 1st Battalion, the Rhodesian African Rifles, from 5 January 1976 to 1 September 1977. During this period the whole unit, including Battalion Headquarters and administrative elements, were spread throughout Rhodesia. Under these difficult conditions, Captain Cracknell re-organized the pay system and his staff. By his dedication and hard work they produced a pay service to the soldiers and their dependants that was exemplary. The contribution this made to the general morale of the unit was considerable. When in barracks, Captain Cracknell worked extremely long hours, far in excess of that normally requited of officers carrying out similar tasks. He also undertook willingly many extra duties for long periods, acting as administrative officer, adjutant and commander of all rear elements in barracks. In addition, when the need arose he drove many miles to deliver pay to troops in the field. His contributions to all other facets of regimental accounting were never neglected, and his experience coupled with his tremendous zeal and determination resulted in an outstanding pay service which earned him the gratitude and undying respect of every member of the unit."*

Warrant Officer Class I T.M.H. KIRRANE

13 April 1979
Major W.M. THOMPSON
Citation: *"Major Wayne Michael Thompson joined the Rhodesian Army in February 1965 and was commissioned in December 1965. After holding various regimental and staff appointments, he was appointed Officer Commanding Headquarter Company, 1st Battalion, The Rhodesian African Rifles in May 1977. In this post he also holds the responsibility of Officer Commanding Battalion Rear Echelon. Since his appointment, the Battalion has been deployed continuously on operations in many parts of Rhodesia and usually far from its base. This necessitated a greater degree of delegation by the commanding officer to Major Thompson. Throughout this very testing period, Major Thompson applied himself enthusiastically to the task, working tirelessly and meticulously to provide the battalion with a sound administrative base and a reliable and efficient back-up system. To achieve this, he worked long hours at night and over weekends. The Battalion, as a major contributor of men and expertise for the army's expansion programme, experienced serious problems in staffing and administration, the adverse effects of which*

were by Major Thompson's resourcefulness and devotion to duty. In his capacity as Officer Commanding Rear Echelon, he has been responsible for the overall administration and well-being of some 2,000 dependents resident within the barracks. This time-consuming and sometimes difficult task was exacerbated by an influx of soldiers' families from tribal areas, bringing new and complex problems. Notwithstanding these additional difficulties and frustrations, Major Thompson showed unflagging dedication in his efforts to maintain the morale and peace of mind of his soldiers. Major Thompson has displayed outstanding devotion to duty in his service to the battalion. His enthusiasm, dedication and personal example in very difficult circumstances have been an inspiration to all who have served with him."

Military Forces Commendation (Operational)
For an act of bravery, distinguished service or continuous devotion to duty
23 October 1970
Lance Corporal S. CHIKAFU
Citation: *"In 1967, L Cpl Simon, then a private, was a member of a combined army/police patrol which made contact with a gang of 21 terrorists. During the action Pte Simon became part of the patrol of a section officer of the BSA Police. While moving, the section officer was wounded. Pte Simon positioned himself behind a tree near the wounded section officer and at regular intervals fired single shots at the enemy to discourage any movement on their part towards the section officer. Approximately one and a half hours later the section officer began to crawl from his position. Pte Simon immediately went to his assistance and, when out of Sight of the enemy, carried the section officer to where a helicopter had landed some distance away. This courageous and exemplary action on the part of Pte Simon is worthy of recognition."*

Warrant Officer Class I A. KORB
Citation: *"Warrant Officer 1st Class Korb displayed courage and determination in evacuating dead and wounded in the face of terrorists. To locate the men, he had to fire a flare which revealed his own position."*

Private T. MAXEN
Citation: *"A fearless and dedicated soldier in several contacts with terrorists, Pte Maxen was on this occasion the machine gunner to a tracker party and, in and exposed position, gave excellent covering fire to permit his party's withdrawal from a greatly superior force. "He is devoted to his machine gun from which he cannot be parted."*

30 October 1970
Corporal S.M. MASHIRI
Citation: *"On an operational patrol, Cpl Mashiri, then a private, with complete disregard for his own safety, displayed great bravery in the face of heavy terrorist fire by crawling to the aid of a wounded comrade and thereby saving his life. By this gallant action, Cpl Mashiri inspired his colleagues and enabled his force to regain the initiative."*

Private J. SIACHOKOLA
Citation: *"Pte Siachokola was a member of a force which engaged a terrorist group in thick bush country. From cover, he saw a comrade crawling to the assistance of a wounded colleague lying in the firing line. Realising that his companion would have difficulty in moving the wounded man on his own, Pte Siachokola, without hesitation or regard for his own life, moved into the area and helped to move the injured man to safety. His display of courage and determination in the face of heavy fire was a prime example of comradeship."*

19 February 1971
Lance Corporal PEDZISAYI

Citation: *"During an operation which took place in Matabeleland in 1967, L Cpl Pedzisayi was wounded in action. Despite being ordered to the rear of the platoon to receive first aid, he remained in the battle area, filling empty magazines and machine gun belts for other members of the platoon. He continued to do this until the end of the action some 20 minutes later when he was given first aid and evacuated by helicopter."*

13 September 1974
Corporal Munangwa GORA

Citation: *"For bravery and devotion to duty. Cpl Munangwa was in command of a section when his platoon became engaged in a contact with a large number of terrorists. Cpl Munangwa was ordered to move to outflank the terrorist position. After a short distance however, his section came under fire from two enemy positions covered by about twelve terrorists. He led his section over a hundred yards of very open ground towards the terrorists and was then pinned down by fire from three other positions. Cpl Munangwa requested assistance from a Provost aircraft and, although heavily engaged with the enemy, he calmly directed the aircraft on to two terrorist positions, thus extricating his men from a difficult situation. Throughout, Cpl Munangwa's courage and leadership were outstanding, and his devotion to duty in carrying out duties was exemplary."*

Lieutenant K.C. JOHNSON

Citation: *"For bravery and devotion to duty. During anti-terrorist operations in the north eastern border area, Lt Johnson, in answer to a request for support, led his platoon, under enemy fire, to the assistance of another platoon. During the ensuing skirmish, Lt Johnson sustained a shrapnel wound. Undaunted, he refused to hand over command and continued to lead his men, showing a high standard of leadership, courage and devotion to duty."*

26 September 1975
Warrant Officer Class II M. HAMANDISHE

Citation: *"For nearly two year and half years, WOII Hamandishe, in the absence of an officer, commanded a platoon on operations. His calmness in times of danger and his outstanding qualities of leadership have, in no small way, contributed to the continual success of his platoon. He has shown commendable initiative and determination and his continuous devotion to duty has been an inspiration to all and men with whom he has served."*

Warrant Officer Class II R. MANGWENDE

Citation: *"During an operation in the north eastern border area, WOII Mangwende suspected a terrorist presence near a certain village. As a result of an intelligent assessment of the situation and his continuous searching and observation of the area, he located a terrorist base. Thereafter he accurately directed air effort on to the occupied terrorist base and, on being reinforced by ground forces, assisted in eliminating the group, resulting in seven killed and a number captured. His astute handling of the situation and his subsequent participation in the battle resulted in an extremely successful encounter."*

Lance Corporal D. MARUVA
Attached to Selous Scouts

Citation: *"Lance Corporal Maruva was involved in seven contacts with terrorists over a period of two and a half years. As a platoon commander's batman for most of that time, he was always directly involved in the fighting. Without exception, L Cpl Maruva has shown initiative and aggression in the face of the enemy in every contact. On one occasion, while operating with another officer, he became involved in a series of running contacts. Throughout this action, L Cpl Maruva distinguished himself by relentlessly and fearlessly pursuing the terrorists from one position to another. He was always to the forefront of his group and never faltered in his willingness to close with the enemy. He was wounded in the final assault of this action and was immediately evacuated. He subsequently recovered and is still on active service."*

Major R.T.O. TILLY
RhSigs, attached RAR

Citation: *"Major R. T. O. Tilly was posted to 1RAR in July 1974, and was appointed company commander of A Company. During an operation, Major Tilly and his stick of three men were uplifted by helicopter from a contact area and dropped some distance away to make contact with a group of terrorists which had been seen by a helicopter pilot. The' group was reported to be between four- and seven-strong. Speed was essential and no reinforcements were at hand. Major Tilly advanced in the general direction of the last sighting. Without warning he found himself a mere ten metres from a group of three heavily armed terrorists. His assessment was swift and accurate. Remaining perfectly cool-headed, he immediately killed the machine gunner who had opened fire on him and then promptly switched his fire to a second terrorist, killing him also. His men killed a third. Still unaware of the exact number of terrorists engaged, Major Tilly led his stick to clear the area. In the process, a fourth terrorist opened fire on Major Tilly but was soon killed."*

Lieutenant M.G.H. WILSON

Citation: *"While Lt Wilson was a platoon commander on Operation Hurricane, he was deployed almost continuously on counter-insurgency operations. He was involved in several contacts with terrorists and on two occasions was fired upon at very close quarters while following up fleeing terrorists. In both these contacts he displayed commendable calmness and a high degree of aggression. The success of his platoon in these and other contacts is in no small way attributable to Lt Wilson's professional and leadership abilities. On one occasion he distinguished himself by leading a long and relentless pursuit of terrorists responsible for the murder of a European farmer and his wife. The follow-up resulted in a contact in which the majority of the terrorists were killed and the remainder captured."*

15 October 1976
Sergeant Z.M. NOKWARA

29 October 1976
Private P. TANDARI

Citation: *"On 24 March 1976, 7 Platoon of C Company 1RAR made contact with a group of terrorists in the operational area. During the contact, Lance Corporal Misheck Dickson was seriously wounded in the stomach and fell in a very vulnerable position. Seeing his predicament, Pte Tandari, with no thought for his own safety, dashed out under fire to assist his comrade. He removed Lance Corporal Dickson's webbing and dragged him to safety. He rendered what first aid he could and informed his platoon commander that an immediate casualty evacuation was necessary. The evacuation was speedily carried out and as a result of Pte Tandari's action Lance Corporal Dickson was able to receive the medical attention he needed."*

23 September 1977
Lieutenant T.M. MOORE

30 November 1979
Warrant Officer Class II M. CHARAMBA
Lieutenant W.T. REVELL

09 February 1979
Private C. NCUBE
Citation: *"For courage and initiative of a high order on a specific operation. His resourcefulness and aggression have set an example to all who have served with him on this and many other operations."*

Military Forces Commendation (Non-operational
For an act of bravery, distinguished service or continuous devotion to duty
11 November 1972
Second Lieutenant A.A. GILLESPIE

11 November 1973
Private V. MACHAYA

29 October 1976
Private P. JACOBE
Citation: *"On 3 April 1976, Pte Jacobe was one of two African soldiers detailed to act as escort on a vehicle belonging to the 10th Battalion of the Rhodesia Regiment. This vehicle, together with another from the same unit, was tasked to uplift troops who had been deployed earlier in the day by helicopter. During the journey, the vehicle on which Pte Jacobe was travelling detonated a landmine and caught fire. He debussed at once with the other escort, Cpl Zinyemba Ranganayi, and they went to the assistance of the driver, whom they found unconscious and strapped in his seat in the burning cab. Fully appreciating that-the vehicle might explode at any moment and the effect that the intense heat would inevitably have on the grenades and ammunition belonging to the driver, Pte Jacobe, with complete disregard for his own safety, assisted Cpl Ranganayi in his attempts to extricate the unconscious man from the vehicle. After a considerable amount of trouble, the two men succeeded in removing the driver from the cab and carried him to safety. During the course of this action, Pte Jacobe tore items of burning clothing from the driver's body with his bare hands, burning his hands and arms in the process. The two men* rendered what limited first aid they could until the arrival of a helicopter which evacuated both the driver and Pte Jacobe, who spent some time in Mtoko hospital, recovering from his burns. The selfless and determined efforts of Pte Jacobe under extremely hazardous circumstances undoubtedly contributed to saving the driver from a gruesome death in the burning vehicle. His actions, particularly in view of his inexperience and short service as a soldier, are worthy of high praise and commendation."*

Corporal R. ZINYEMBA
Citation: *"On 3 April 1976, Cpl Ranganayi was detailed together with Pte Phineas Jacobe, to act as escort on a vehicle belonging to the 10th Battalion of the Rhodesia Regiment. This vehicle, with another from the same unit, was tasked to uplift troops who had been deployed earlier in the day by helicopter. During the course of the journey, the vehicle in which Cpl Ranganayi was travelling detonated a landmine. After the initial shock of the explosion, Cpl Ranganayi, accompanied by Pte Jacobe, debussed from the vehicle which had caught fire. They hurried forward to see if the driver was all right, only to find that he was unconscious in the driving seat and that the vehicle cab was on fire. They attempted to pull the diver out of the burning vehicle but discovered that his seat belt was still securely fastened round his waist. Fully aware of the very strong possibility that the vehicle might explode at any moment and the effect that the intense heat of the burning engine would inevitably have on the grenades and ammunition belonging to the driver, Cpl Ranganayi, with complete disregard for his own safety, climbed into the burning vehicle cab and unfastened the driver's safety belt. Then with the aid of Pte Jacobe, Cpl Ranganayi pulled the unconscious soldier from the vehicle and carried him to a point of safety some fifty paces away. Here the two men tore items of burning clothing from the driver's body and rendered what limited first aid they could. The driver was evacuated by helicopter, but regrettably died some days later as a result of his burns. Cpl Ranganayi's selfless and determined efforts under extremely hazardous circumstances undoubtedly saved the driver from a gruesome death in the burning vehicle and are worthy of high praise and commendation."*

11 November 1978
Private C. CHAMUNORWA
Lieutenant J.W. HARDY

11 November 1977
Warrant Officer Class II P.H. HORSBOROUGH

2nd Battalion Rhodesian African Rifles

Silver Cross of Rhodesia (SCR)

For conspicuous gallantry

13 October 1978

Second Lieutenant B. M. THOMPSON (Posthumous)

Citation: *"Lieutenant Thompson joined the Second Battalion RAR in March 1977. He was involved in over thirty-five contacts in which more than 170 terrorists were killed. On twenty-nine occasions he parachuted into the contact area, often in high winds and into hazardous dropping zones. On 12 September 1977, Thompson and four patrols were flown by helicopter into a narrow valley from which fire had been directed at the aircraft. Hardly had they been deployed when the aircraft was called away to another incident and Thompson was left in command with no air support. In a series of sweeps through rocky terrain in which there were many natural caves, eight terrorists and twelve terrorist recruits were wiped out. During the action Thompson suspected that a terrorist was hiding in a very narrow crevice in the rock face. Taking off his webbing, he squeezed into the crevice and was engaged with a terrorist at such close range that he actually struck the terrorist's rifle aside as he was firing. As the terrorist tried to escape, Lieutenant Thompson shot him dead as well as three other terrorists. On 27 February 1978, Thompson killed three terrorists while charging at the head of his men into thick bush under heavy fire. On 4 March 1978, he eliminated three of the thirteen terrorists killed by his company, once again in thick, rough country with the encounters taking place at point blank range. On 6 June 1978, eight terrorists and fifty recruits were contacted in thick bush. Thompson's patrol accounted for most of the enemy group. Once again, he led his men at the double in the face of fire from the terrorists. He advanced so quickly that he almost ran into supporting fire from the air in his determination to close with and destroy the enemy. On 27 June 1978, Thompson's patrol was ordered to sweep an area in which at least three terrorists were known to be hiding. Almost immediately they came under heavy close-range fire and the machine gunner was badly wounded. Still under fire, Thompson moved forward and dragged the wounded man to cover. He then led his patrol forward and killed two of the enemy. However in the ensuing chase, Thompson and one of his men were killed."*

14 September 1979

Corporal A. ALI

Citation: *"Over the period February 1978 to February 1979, Corporal Ali has been involved in numerous contacts with terrorists. In all of these engagements, Corporal Ali has shown outstanding leadership and his determination to close with and kill the enemy has been an inspiration to all. He has personally killed fifteen terrorists and captured four. On 16 July 1978, Corporal Ali approached what he thought was a dead terrorist. The terrorist sprang to life and gripped the barrel of Corporal Ali's rifle, trying to wrest it from him. Although Corporal Ali could have pulled the trigger and killed the terrorist, instead he calmly drew his pistol and ordered the terrorist to surrender, which he did. The captured terrorist proved to be a section commander and much valuable information was gleaned from him, leading to several other contacts. On 26 October 1978, during the mopping-up stages of a Fireforce action, two terrorists opened fire on Corporal Ali's group of soldiers, wounding one of them. The terrorists were lodged in a thickly-wooded riverbed with steep banks. Corporal Ali borrowed a machine gun from another soldier and with his platoon commander jumped into the riverbed. One terrorist was quickly killed. Corporal Ali saw the second terrorist about to throw a hand grenade and tried to fire at him. His machine gun, however, did not fire due to a stoppage. Although he was completely exposed to the terrorist, he calmly gave an indication to his platoon commander who was able to kill the terrorist. Undoubtedly, his exceptional calm and discipline saved both his life and that of his platoon commander. On 9 February 1979, Corporal Ali was in command of a sweep line moving through dense bush, known to contain terrorists. In a most aggressive manner, he led his men through the bush and into contact with the terrorists, accounting for the whole group. He personally killed one terrorist and captured a further two. On 20 February 1979, Corporal Ali, while deploying at night, heard firing. Acting on his own initiative, he re-deployed his patrol towards the firing. At first light the following morning he observed suspicious movement some distance from his position. Arming himself with a pistol and accompanied by one other soldier, he observed a group of seven terrorists. He returned to his original position and called for the Fireforce. While awaiting their arrival, he re-positioned his patrol to cut off the terrorist escape routes. After an exceptionally good talk-on to the Fireforce, he calmly controlled the ground forces throughout the highly successful action. Throughout these and other engagements, Corporal Ali has consistently shown complete disregard for his own safety. His tactical skill and high degree of aggression throughout have inspired his men and largely been responsible for his sub-unit's considerable successes."*

Lieutenant A.T. TELFER

Citation: *"Lieutenant Andrew Thomas Telfer joined the Second Battalion RAR in February 1977 as a platoon commander. Since that date he has been deployed almost continually on counter-insurgency operations. Over the period June 1978 to December 1978, Lieutenant Telfer was involved in numerous contacts with terrorists. Since then, he has again been involved in many contacts, both as a ground-force commander and as an airborne commander. In all engagements he has displayed considerable initiative, outstanding leadership and distinguished personal conduct. Under his direction, more than forty terrorists have been eliminated and his personal bravery has been an inspiration of the highest order. On 5 June 1978, Lieutenant Telfer and three men were deployed into a Fireforce action by helicopter. Whilst sweeping through the area, he and his men came under heavy fire from two terrorists lodged in a rocky outcrop. Despite two air strikes, the terrorists continued to direct heavy and accurate fire on Lieutenant's position. With no regard for his personal safety, Lieutenant Telfer led an attack on the terrorist position and although being fired at from less than ten metres, he personally killed one terrorist. The other fled but was re-located, wounded, in a nearby field. Without hesitation Lieutenant Telfer ran across the open field, and although again being subjected to fire from the terrorist, killed him. On 26 October 1978, Lieutenant Telfer parachuted into a Fireforce operation. On landing he badly injured his ankle which was subsequently placed into a plaster cast for several weeks. Despite his injury, Lieutenant Telfer continued to lead his men throughout the three-hour operation and was directly responsible for the deaths of four of the six terrorists killed. During the mopping-up phase Lieutenant Telfer's patrol came under heavy fire from two terrorists hiding in a thickly wooded river line. One of his men was wounded and repeated attempts to dislodge the terrorists failed. Again, with no regard for his personal safety, and in considerable pain from his injured ankle, lieutenant Telfer jumped into the river bed with one of his men and, although under heavy fire the whole time, personally killed both terrorists. On 13 November 1978, he was again deployed into a Fireforce action by helicopter. He was immediately subjected to heavy fire from the terrorist position. With commendable coolness, he directed an air strike on to the terrorists and then led an attack on to their position. All five terrorists were killed. At last light on 2 February 1979, returning from a successful Fireforce engagement, Lieutenant Telfer and three men were re-deployed to a sighting of ten terrorists. Shortly after being dropped, he sent two of his three men to cut off any terrorists attempting to escape from the contact area. Lieutenant Telfer and one man then ran into the kraal in which the main terrorist group was situated. In fading light, Lieutenant Telfer killed two terrorists and several recruits. Throughout these and numerous other contacts, Lieutenant Telfer's personal courage, exemplary leadership and aggressive attitude have inspired all those with whom he has been in action."*

Second Lieutenant G.L. TRASS

Citation: *"Second Lieutenant Graeme Leslie Trass has served as a platoon commander in the Second Battalion, the Rhodesian African Rifles since March 1978. During this time he has been involved in numerous contacts and has been responsible for the elimination of a large number of terrorists. On 10 August 1978, Second Lieutenant Trass and a patrol of four men were parachuted into a contact area during a Fireforce action. Immediately after landing, he led a sweep line towards the terrorist position. Contact was made and all six terrorists were killed. Afterwards a patrol of four men was pinned down in open ground by four terrorists hiding in a rocky outcrop. Second Lieutenant Trass and three men were directed to assist. Without hesitation, he led the patrol across the open ground and skirmished through the terrorists' position, the whole time being subjected to intense terrorist fire. In all, four terrorists were killed. In this engagement, a total of ten terrorists were eliminated, due largely to the coolness and leadership of Second Lieutenant Trass. On 28 August 1978, a patrol of four men, commanded by an officer, was fired on by two terrorists at very close range. The officer was wounded and the patrol forced to withdraw in the face of heavy fire. Repeated air attacks failed to dislodge the terrorists. Second Lieutenant Trass and one man skirmished across open ground under fire, and assaulted the terrorist position, killing both terrorists at close quarters. On 7 December 1978, a patrol of four men was fired upon by three terrorists entrenched in a narrow and thickly-wooded re-entrant. The officer was wounded and the patrol forced to withdraw. Subsequent air attacks failed to eliminate the terrorists. Second Lieutenant Trass, leading seven men, attempted to sweep through the terrorist position. At ten metres' range, the terrorists fired upon his men, seriously wounding the machine gunner, who fell within a few yards of the terrorists. His men were forced to withdraw to cover. In the fading light, and believing that the machine gunner was still alive, Second Lieutenant Trass crawled forward and extricated him, under fire from within a few metres of the terrorist, showing great personal courage in so doing. On these and other occasions, Second Lieutenant Trass has shown disregard for his own safety, displaying courage and aggressive leadership of the highest order. His conduct has been an inspiration to all who have served with him."*

05 October 1976
Lance Corporal R. HARIORI

Citation: *"For the past three and a half years, Lance-Corporal Raymond Hariori has been deployed almost continuously on counter-insurgency operations. He has had numerous contacts with terrorists, most of which have been while he was a member of the Fireforce. In all contacts, Lance-Corporal Hariori has displayed outstanding leadership and determination to close with and kill the enemy. On 10 August 1978, he was a member of a patrol commanded by an officer. The patrol was called upon to assist another group which was pinned down in open ground by a group of terrorists in a rocky outcrop. Taking a machine gun from another soldier, he and his platoon commander assaulted the terrorist position. Lance-Corporal Hariori personally killed two of the terrorists. On 28 August 1978, Lance-Corporal Hariori was in a sweep line when they came under fire from two terrorists hidden in thick bush. Despite the heavy and accurate fire from the terrorist position, Lance-Corporal Hariori and his platoon commander skirmished across open ground and killed both terrorists at very close range. On 13 February 1979, during a Fireforce action, Lance-Corporal Hariori and his patrol were tasked to clear an area of thick cover, known to contain terrorists. In a swift and aggressive manner he led his patrol through the cover and eliminated three terrorists. On the same day, and in another Fireforce action, he and his patrol were deployed by helicopter after two terrorists had been seen from the air. In fading light and followed by his men, Lance Corporal Hariori tracked the two terrorists into re-entrant where he personally killed one and captured the other. This was the fourth time that day that he had been deployed into action, having started at dawn. On 7 March 1979, Lance-Corporal Hariori again led his men in an exceptionally aggressive manner against a terrorist group, eliminating two terrorists. Throughout these and many other contacts, Lance-Corporal Hariori has shown a total disregard for personal danger. His conspicuous gallantry, fine leadership and personal aggression have earned him great respect among his fellow soldiers."*

30 June 1980
Corporal A. MATAMBO

Citation: *"Corporal Alois Matambo joined the Second Battalion, the Rhodesian African Rifles, in August 1976. Since then he has been deployed almost continuously on operations and has been in numerous contacts with terrorists During the night of 30 March 1979, Cpl Matambo led a patrol of four men to investigate a beer-drink. Cover was sparse, so he and his men crawled over open ground to within 30 metres of the gathering. Simultaneously, the beer finished and dispersing locals saw the patrol and ran away, shouting to warn the terrorists who were present. The terrorists opened fire on the exposed patrol. Cpl Matambo immediately led an assault directly at the terrorists. One terrorist was killed and another wounded. Both weapons were recovered. On 5 April 1979 Cpl Matambo and his patrol of three men, while occupying an observation post, sighted a group of terrorists based up in very thick bush. As the Fireforce was not available to react, Cpl Matambo led his patrol off the hill in an attempt to contact the terrorists. Seeing that the area around the thick bush in which the terrorists were based was open, Cpl Matambo led a charge across the open ground. On breaking cover his patrol was seen and fired on by the terrorists, who then ran away. Cpl Matambo succeeded in killing the terrorist in command of the group. Others were wounded or escaped. In this action, Cpl Matambo's determination to kill the enemy was particularly praiseworthy as he knew at the outset he was heavily outnumbered. On the 10 November 1979, Cpl Matambo and his patrol were ambushed from three separate positions at thirty metres' range, by a group of ten terrorists. The patrol was caught in the open with no cover. Totally disregarding his own safety, Cpl Matambo charged the main terrorist position and personally killed three terrorists. He then controlled the ensuing firefight which resulted in a further two terrorists being killed and two wounded. Among those killed were the platoon commander and platoon security officer. Throughout these and other actions, Cpl Matambo has consistently shown outstanding leadership, personal courage and a high degree of aggression. His actions have earned him the respect and admiration of the members of his unit."*

Officer of the Order of the Legion of Merit (OLM)

For distinguished service to Rhodesia
23 September 1977
Major N.G.C. FAWCETT BCR

Citation: *"Major Fawcett and his company transferred en bloc from 1RAR to 2RAR shortly after the formation of the latter in 1975. Fawcett has been deeply involved on two occasions, and in separate areas, in planning and executing major operations designed to assist the administration in controlling the population. On the first operation, in the north eastern area, Major Fawcett and his company, with the support of the civil authorities, developed a massive protected village complex and turned it into a functional and self-supporting area. In terrain and weather conditions completely adverse to operations, and under considerable harassment from terrorists and hostile Mozambicans, he again played a major part in protecting the population and restoring a large degree of stability and normality in the area. This enabled the economy of the area to become viable again. Also during this period, he frequently led his men on the ground in action against the terrorists."*

Member of the Order of the Legion of Merit (MLM)

For distinguished service to Rhodesia
23 September 1977
Major A. DENNISON BCR

Citation: *"Major André Dennison has been a company commander in 2RAR since its formation in late 1975. The successes the company has had are due, in no small part, to the tireless efforts of Major Dennison. Displaying absolute dedication to the task, he has developed a first-class operational fighting force. On many occasions he has himself led his company, or elements of it, into contacts with terrorists, showing to them all determination required in combating the terrorist menace."*

11 November 1978
Warrant Officer Class I L.C. HALLAMORE

Citation: *"Regimental Sergeant Major Hallamore joined the army in May 1961 as one of the original members of the RLI. He served in the successive ranks of private to warrant officer 2nd class, becoming one of the youngest warrant officers in the army. In 1973, he was posted to the School of Infantry as an instructor and was appointed Company Sergeant Major of the cadet wing. Many a young officer owes his high standard of training to the diligence of Warrant Officer Hallamore. On the 1 January 1976, he was posted to the Second Battalion, the Rhodesian African Rifles as its first Regimental Sergeant Major, where his is still serving. He was faced with many difficult and frustrating problems. These varied from a lack of accommodation for troops, the storage, accounting and care of ammunition with no facilities whatsoever, and the lack of any proper barracks complex. The problems of discipline in a new unit were handled decisively by Regimental Sergeant Major Hallamore. He has shown unflagging enthusiasm and dedication to his duties and his untiring efforts to improve the security of the temporary camp and the new barracks have been most impressive. He has built up the unit Regimental Police into a highly efficient body of men. Although outside the scope of his normal duties, Regimental Sergeant Major Hallamore has assisted in training the 81mm Mortar and Anti-Tank Platoons. Without his efforts these platoons would not have achieved their present high standards. He has on several occasions accompanied the Mortar Platoon on operations under difficult and trying circumstances. Regimental Sergeant-Major Hallamore's ability, devotion to duty and exemplary conduct have been worthy of the highest praise."*

30 June 1980
Warrant Officer Class II A. CHIMUTI

Bronze Cross of Rhodesia (BCR)
For gallantry
29 July 1977
Lieutenant G.J. SCHRAG

Citation: *"On 31 October 1976, a platoon led by Lt Schrag was involved in a two-phase, set-piece attack on two enemy camps, each of which included a large group of terrorists. Despite coming under heavy fire from the first camp, Lt Schrag led the assault with 'great determination', forcing the enemy to break and run. Having secured the first camp, the platoon swept through the second camp, coming under close-range fire from two terrorists who had hidden in a riverbed beyond the camp. The platoon went to ground, but Lt Schrag charged into the riverbed alone and killed both terrorists at a range of less than ten metres. He then led his platoon in a sweep of very thick cover where a further four terrorists were killed. Enemy small arms and mortar fire was intense throughout the engagement."*

07 October 1977
Warrant Officer Class II V. RASHAYI

Citation: *"In March 1976, after a long follow-up, his platoon came under fire from a group of terrorists. In the opening burst, WOII Rashayi was hit in the leg. Despite his wound, he returned fire, drove a terrorist from cover and killed him as he turned to run. His stick then killed a second terrorist before the rest of the terrorists fled. His company, involved in another long follow-up, came under fire, and WOII Rashayi led his stick into the attack. All the terrorists were killed. In October 1976, WOII Rashayi killed a terrorist with a grenade. In 1977, WOII Rashayi's stick wounded and captured a terrorist from whom valuable intelligence was gained. In February 1977, he initiated a contact near a kraal by shooting the enemy section leader through the leg and killing the terrorist next to him."*

13 October 1978
Lieutenant A.R.M. THRUSH

Citation: *"Since joining the 2nd Battalion, the Rhodesian African Rifles, in November 1977, Lieutenant Thrush has been involved in no fewer than 25 Fireforce contacts which accounted for more than ninety terrorists. In every deployment he has been the first man on the ground and usually the first to make contact. With his coolness under fire and his knack of accurately assessing the situation, he has led his men in exemplary fashion, eliminating a large number of terrorists. On 13 April 1978, four terrorists were trapped in a cave. During attempts to get them to surrender, Lieutenant Thrush, with complete disregard for his safety, entered the mouth of the cave and shot and wounded one terrorist. At this, two other terrorists promptly surrendered and the fourth was killed. On 22 April 1978, a similar situation developed and again Lieutenant Thrush took considerable personal risk in clearing several caves with grenades. All these contacts took place during the rainy season when the cover was extremely thick and most encounters took place at ranges well under ten metres. At no time did he allow himself to be deterred and his courageous example and determination to kill the enemy were at all times an inspiration to his soldiers."*

09 February 1979
Major A. DENNISON MLM

Citation: *"During October 1978, Major Dennison was severely wounded in the initial stages of a contact. With a shattered femur and extensive bleeding from his wounds, he lost consciousness. On regaining consciousness, he refused evacuation and continued to direct the battle in a calm and competent manner. After one hour and fifteen minutes, he was taken out of the area, semi-conscious from loss of blood. The contact was extremely successful owing to Major Dennison's bravery and dedication to his task under circumstances far beyond the normal call of duty. Within the year, this brave soldier was to pay the ultimate cost."*

14 September 1979
Lance Corporal H. MAWIRE

Citation: *"Since joining the Second Battalion, the Rhodesian African Rifles, Lance Corporal Mawire has been deployed almost continuously on operations and has been in contact with terrorists over thirty times. On all occasions he has displayed a high degree of aggression and determination to close with and kill the enemy. On 24 and 25 March 1978, during extended contacts with terrorists, he personally killed seven terrorists with his machine gun, the whole time being exposed to retaliatory fire. Again, on the 25 March 1978, he forced a terrorist to surrender by firing his machine gun at his feet and finally shooting the terrorist's rifle out of his hands. On 5 September 1978, during a Fireforce action, Lance-Corporal Mawire's patrol, while crossing a dry riverbed, was fired upon from the opposite bank by two terrorists. As the rest of the patrol sought what meagre cover was available, Lance-Corporal Mawire coolly stood in the riverbed, exposed to the terrorists' fire, and killed both terrorists by firing his machine gun from the hip, thereby saving his patrol almost certain casualties. On the 19 September 1978, while acting as second-in-command to an officer, the sweep line in which he was a member was held up by the fire of two terrorists. Without orders, and disregarding his own personal safety, Lance-Corporal Mawire moved forward and killed both terrorists. Throughout these and other actions, Lance-Corporal Mawire has displayed maturity, a high degree of aggression and a total disregard for his own safety. His gallant and efficient conduct is an outstanding example to the rest of his company."*

05 October 1979
Private G. MPONDA

Citation: *"Private George Mponda has served with the Second Battalion, the Rhodesian African Rifles since 16 August 1978. During this period he has been involved in numerous contacts with terrorists. On 28 March*

1979, he was a member of an eight-man patrol occupying an observation post. He was positioned as a sentry on the eastern side of the feature with the other members occupying positions on the south and west sides of the same feature. At 1300 hours, the patrol commander moved forward of Private Mponda's position. Shortly after the patrol commander was out of sight, Private Mponda heard a single shot followed by heavy bursts of fire. Carrying his machine gun, Private Mponda ran down the hill towards the firing. Private Mponda saw his patrol commander lying wounded on the ground. A terrorist, with bayonet fixed to his rifle, was approaching the patrol commander. A further twenty-five terrorists, in extended line, were advancing up the feature. At that time they were approximately twenty metres forward of his position, which was completely exposed. Without hesitation and with total disregard for his own personal safety, Private Mponda opened fire on the terrorist approaching his patrol commander and then fired at the oncoming terrorist group. Simultaneously, the terrorists fired at him, many rounds striking the ground around his feet. Private Mponda remained where he was and continued to fire at the advancing terrorists. In the face of his determined and effective opposition, the terrorists broke off their attack and fled down the hillside. Private Mponda then gave covering fire while two other members of his patrol, who had come to his assistance, removed the patrol commander. Subsequent information confirmed that Private Mponda had wounded two of the terrorists. From the terrorists' actions, it is certain that they were mounting an assault on the observation post. In addition to saving the life of his patrol commander, Private Mponda's lone and determined action was an act of outstanding bravery."

Corporal C. NCUBE

Citation: *"Corporal Calvin Ncube is a section commander in the Second Battalion, the Rhodesian African Rifles. Over the past 18 months he has been in over fifteen contacts with terrorists which have resulted in a large number being eliminated. Throughout all these engagements, Corporal Ncube has displayed a high degree of personal courage and determination to close with and kill the enemy. On 31 March 1978, Corporal Ncube and his men were involved in a Fireforce action against a large number of terrorists and recruits. Shortly after making contact the K-car became unserviceable and no air support was available. One terrorist broke cover and attempted to escape. The terrorist break-out was indicated to Corporal Ncube by the helicopter pilot. Corporal Ncube, leading his men, sprinted after the terrorist. After a distance of about six hundred metres Corporal Ncube sighted the terrorist running into thick cover. Despite a heavy and accurate burst of fire from the terrorist, which came very close to hitting him, Corporal Ncube continued to give chase and, having outstripped his men and on the point of exhaustion, closed with and killed the terrorist at close range. Immediately after this action, Corporal Ncube and his men were re-directed to the main terrorist position where six terrorists were killed. Throughout this action Corporal Ncube again displayed a high standard of leadership and aggression. On 28 August 1978, during the mopping-up stages of a Fireforce action, Corporal Ncube and three men were directed towards an escaping terrorist. Again leading his men at the run and outstripping them, he finally forced the terrorist to halt and take cover. Without hesitation and completely disregarding the fire directed at him, Corporal Ncube advanced and killed the terrorist at close range. In these and other engagements, Corporal Ncube has displayed total disregard for his own personal safety and has shown outstanding leadership. His aggressive attitude is held in the highest esteem by all who serve with him."*

Second Lieutenant C.J.E. VINCENT

Citation: *"Second Lieutenant Christopher James Edward Vincent joined the Second Battalion, The Rhodesian African Rifles, as a platoon commander in March 1978. Since that time he has been involved in 30 contacts during which his company eliminated 200 terrorists. In all his contacts Second Lieutenant Vincent has displayed commendable coolness and a high degree of aggression which have contributed directly to the successes of his sub-*

unit. In his first contact, Second Lieutenant Vincent killed the only terrorist accounted for. Shortly afterwards he was concussed by a terrorist grenade which exploded within one yard of him which permanently damaged his ear-drums. Within 24 hours he was again in action and personally killed three of the seven terrorists killed by his company. On 26 April 1978, Second Lieutenant Vincent, through his tactical handling of a difficult situation in very thick bush, was responsible for the killing of four terrorists and the capture of two others. On 9 October 1978, he parachuted into action against a large number of terrorists and terrorist recruits. He injured his neck when landing, but despite the acute pain, remained in control of the ground forces for several hours, during which numerous and intense firefights with terrorists took place. Largely due to his aggression and fine command ability, 20 terrorists and a large number of their recruits were killed in action. On 15 October 1978, Second Lieutenant Vincent was leading a patrol of three men when they were fired on by two terrorists at very close range. Both machine-guns jammed, leaving Second Lieutenant Vincent with the only weapon in the patrol. Although in extreme danger, he stood his ground and calmly returned the fire, killing both terrorists and thus saving his own life and those of the other two members of his patrol. Throughout his operational service, Second Lieutenant Vincent has shown outstanding leadership and a high degree of tactical skill. His personal courage and aggression have inspired all those who have served with him."

30 June 1980
Private C. MUSIIWA

Defence Forces Medal for Meritorious Service (DMM)

For meritorious service
11 November 1977
Captain C.D. FERGUSON
Warrant Officer Class I K.C. MUCHINGURI

11 November 1978
Temporary Major J.D. IRVINE
RhAMC attached 2RAR

Citation: *"Major Irvine was posted to 2RAR on its formation, as its first medical officer. He was responsible for setting up medical services within the unit under difficult and trying circumstances. His treatment, in the field, of operational casualties has always been of a high professional standard and by his devotion to duty he has saved many lives."*

Captain A.F. LOGAN

Citation: *"Captain Logan was appointed administrative officer of the newly formed Battalion in 1976 when he immediately undertook the arduous task of organising the entire administrative system. This task was an extremely difficult one. Captain Logan's ability in the administrative field is of the highest order and the present efficiency of the unit administration is due mainly to this officer's resourcefulness and devotion to duty."*

Warrant Officer Class II T. MUFANEBADZA

Citation: *"WOII Mufanebadza has completed 23 years' service with the army, the majority of which has been on operational duties. In 1976 he was posted to the Second Battalion and appointed Company Sergeant Major of a newly formed company. In this position he had the task of moulding a company of new recruits and newly posted non-commissioned officers into a disciplined force. He achieved all that his demanding task required of him, and more. The attention devoted by him to all aspects of his work contributed in no small way to the overall efficiency and high morale of the company."*

13 April 1979
Warrant Officer Class II M. HAMANDISHE
Citation: *"WOII Hamandishe served with 1RAR from the time he attested into the army in 1958 until he was appointed company sergeant-major of the newly formed B Company of the 2nd Battalion in 1975. During this time he was actively involved in counter-insurgency operations. Throughout his twenty-one years in the army WOII Hamandishe's service has been characterised by outstanding conduct and devotion to duty."*

Warrant Officer Class II A.W. PIRIE
RhAMC attached 2RAR
Citation: *"WOII Pirie's has been characterized by devotion to duty, a high standard of professional expertise and a willingness to accept responsibility. Since joining the Rhodesian Army Medical Corps in 1959 he has served that corps, and at the Rhodesian Air Force base at Thornhill, Gwelo. He has served with the 1st Battalion RAR on operational duties and was posted to the 2nd Battalion in 1975 as its first Ward Master. Under adverse conditions, he has assisted in the formation of, and controlled the day-to-day functions of the military wards at Fort Victoria, Chiredzi and latterly, the emergency ward within Masvingo Barracks. In addition he has spent long periods attached to operational headquarters in the field where he has contributed directly to the morale of the soldiers."*

Military Forces Commendation (Operational)

For an act of bravery, distinguished service or continuous devotion to duty
15 October 1976
Sergeant Z.M. NOKWARA
Citation: *"For the past three years, Sergeant Zwidzayi M. Nokwara, formerly of 1RAR, has been with the 2nd Battalion RAR. He has been engaged in continuous anti-terrorist operations as a Section Commander. Although not a young man, he has consistently displayed aggression and determination of a high order when in action. In numerous engagements against terrorists in which a number have been killed and others captured, Sergeant Nokwara's calmness and courage have been an inspiration to his men. His sense of humour in adversity and his leadership and tenacity under fire have resulted in noteworthy successes for his platoon and section in particular. His professionalism and unswerving allegiance are a constant example to all who serve with him."*

29 July 1977
Warrant Officer Class II B. MAKURIRA

23 September 1977
Lieutenant J.A.Q. VOS

27 January 1978
Private M. MUCHANYU
Second Lieutenant A.T. TELFER

31 March 1978
Major A. DENNISON
Citation: *"In August 1977, Major Andre Dennison was in command of a unit which killed five terrorists and captured one during a contact. However one terrorist managed to escape into a cave. Despite several attempts to flush him out of the cave, the terrorist managed to find an excellent position to secure himself and to maintain a barrage of heavy and accurate fire upon the Security Force team. The next day a number of further attempts were made to dislodge the determined terrorist, all to no avail. Major Dennison and two other men then entered the cave via an inclined shaft. The terrorist was concealed in another part of the cave and opened fire on the three intruders, wounding one of them. Major Dennison dragged the injured man clear with the help of the other soldier. Under heavy fire they managed to get him out of the cave. Eventually the terrorist, who was accompanied by a woman, was smoked out and he surrendered."*

13 October 1978
Corporal C. CHINGOMBE
Lance Corporal P. MUGWAGWA
Private D. NJOVO
Lance Corporal D. TAKAWIRA

14 September 1979
Warrant Officer Class II W. RWAZIVESU

15 October 1979
Acting Sergeant S. RUFURA

Military Forces Commendation (Non-operational)

For an act of bravery, distinguished service or continuous devotion to duty
11 November 1976
Corporal K. ZVINOITAVAMWE
Citation: *"On 2 February 1976, an exploding gas cylinder started a serious fire which spread to a vehicle which was loaded with various types of ammunition. Without any consideration for his own safety, Cpl Zvinoitavamwe climbed into the cab of the blazing vehicle and drove it about 50 metres away from the original source of the fire and another vehicle which had also been nearby. Shortly after he left the vehicle, the ammunition in the back started exploding, completely gutting the back of the vehicle and smashing the rear windows of the driver's cab. Had Cpl Zvinoitavamwe been in the cab at the time, he would undoubtedly have been severely injured if not killed. Cpl Zvinoitavamwe's actions were on his own initiative and he had received no orders to act in the manner in which he did. By his action he helped to save equipment from destruction and saved the other fire fighters from almost certain serious injuries."*

Depot and Independent Companies

Bronze Cross of Rhodesia (BCR)

For gallantry

11 November 1978

Sergeant T.O. NEL

1 (Indep) Coy

Citation: "*Temporary Sergeant Theodore Owen Nel is the Tracker Platoon commander operating in support of 1 and 4 (Independent) Companies, Rhodesian African Rifles. On 26 August 1977 Sergeant Nel was in command of a six-man patrol following up a group of terrorists estimated to be between eight and 12 in number when the patrol came under heavy fire from close range. Sergeant Nel immediately engaged the enemy, killing one of the sentries and forcing the terrorists to abandon their positions. Sergeant Nel and his patrol pursued the terrorists for twenty-five minutes before locating a recently vacated resting place where they found thirty-four packs which had been abandoned by the terrorists, While recovering these, the patrol again came under heavy fire from the terrorist group, now estimated to be over thirty. A fierce firefight ensued with the terrorists intent on driving off the numerically smaller patrol. Sergeant Nel and his men refused to be driven from their positions, despite the fact that ammunition was running dangerously low. Because of this Sergeant Nel decided to utilize a terrorist rocket launcher which he had seen among the terrorist packs in the open riverbed. With little regard for his own personal safety he made two forays under heavy automatic fire and recovered both the launcher and ammunition. Sergeant Nel then moved to a position from where he engaged the main enemy concentration with accurate fire. The terrorists broke contact and fled, abandoning a large quantity of material, including eighteen landmines. There is no doubt that Sergeant Nel's brave and calculated actions forced the terrorists to abandon their positions and saved what could have been a dangerous situation for his patrol. This action typifies the courage, determination and skill that Sergeant Nel has consistently displayed throughout his service. His resolute pursuit of the enemy has resulted in his being involved in a large number of successful contacts in the past two years.*"

01 December 1978

Major D.H. PRICE

1 (Indep) Coy

Citation: "*Major Price has shown courage and initiative of a high order during a long period of operations. His devotion to duty and aggressive actions have set an excellent example to the men under his command.*"

Defence Forces Medal for Meritorious Service (DMM)

11 November 1978

Major P.J. MORRIS

Depot RAR

Citation: "*Major Morris was appointed as officer commanding on the opening of the Depot, the Rhodesian African Rifles, on 1 December 1973. Initially the Depot only had a small staff, and only a limited number of recruits passed through this establishment. In August 1977, however, operational requirements dictated that the output of trainees be greatly increased to provide soldiers for the Independent Companies, the Rhodesian African Rifles and the battalions of the Rhodesia Regiment. To meet this requirement the Depot had to expand to accommodate 1,200 recruits with a monthly throughput of 400 men. A very much condensed syllabus was also introduced to reduce the training period. Major Morris set about the reorganisation of the Depot with tremendous energy, determination and the enthusiasm of a truly professional soldier. His refusal to accept defeat enabled him to overcome the many training and administrative problems such as shortages of staff, equipment, buildings and other much needed facilities. His high standard of leadership and moral courage inspired the Depot staff to meet the challenge and so provide trained soldiers for field units.*"

13 April 1979

Warrant Class II G.D.P. MORGAN

6 (Indep) Coy

Citation: "*WOII George David Peter Morgan was appointed to the post of company sergeant-major of 6 (Indep) Company RAR on the formation of that unit in September 1976. Since his appointment, won Morgan has exhibited an untiring, enthusiastic and dedicated approach towards all his duties, often to the detriment of his personal life. He has spared no effort in personally supervising and guiding his inexperienced subordinates to achieve a high standard of efficiency, discipline and professionalism in all their activities. In late 1977, he was in command of a small group of his company during the temporary absence of their commander. This group was attacked by an overwhelming number of terrorists who carried out a determined and prolonged assault which included heavy mortar, rocket and small-arms fire. Despite the weight of the enemy fire and casualties to his men, won Morgan often exposed himself to the enemy to assist these casualties and rally his men to drive off the enemy. That his small group was able to do so, was undoubtedly due to the determined and calm leadership shown by WOII Morgan in extremely hazardous circumstances. In subsequent encounters with the enemy, won Morgan has continued to show a high standard of calm discipline and steadiness which have been an example to all who serve with him. His strong sense of discipline and constant striving for efficiency, have also been notable in a non-operational context, to the extent of attracting favourable comment from other service personnel, all of which have brought credit not only to himself but also his unit and the army as a whole.*"

Military Forces Commendation (Operational)

For an act of bravery, distinguished service or continuous devotion to duty

1979

Sergeant J.G.F. STEYN

6 (Indep) Coy

Citation: "*Sergeant Johannes Gerhardus Frederick Steyn joined 6 (Indep) Company RAR in October 1977 as a platoon sergeant. His continuous devotion to duty and dedication to the elimination of terrorists set an outstanding example to the inexperienced African and European soldiers in his sub-unit. Sergeant Steyn frequently proposed new plans by which he could outwit the enemy, and always insisted on leading such ventures himself. His determined leadership eventually resulted in the elimination, at close range, of three terrorists on the night of 30 June 1978. Sergeant Steyn was injured in this contact, and was personally responsible for killing all three of the enemy. In spite of the injury sustained in this contact, Sergeant Steyn insisted on returning to active duties as soon as he had been released from hospital, despite suffering discomfort and pain. His continuous devotion to duty is indeed an inspiration and example to all members of his unit.*"

Victoria Cross
(VC)

Most Excellent
Order of the British
Empire Officer of
the Military Division
(OBE)

Most Excellent
Order of the British
Empire Member of
the Military Division
(MBE)

Imperial Service
Order
(ISO)

Military Cross
WWI
(MC)

Military Cross
WWII
(MC)

Distinguished
Conduct Medal
WWI
(DCM)

Distinguished
Conduct Medal
WWII
(DCM)

Military Medal
WWI
(MM)

Military Medal
WWII
(MM)

Mentioned In
Dispatches Oak
Leaf device
1914–20
(MiD)

Mentioned In
Dispatches Oak
Leaf device
1939–1945
(MiD)

Officer of the
Legion of Merit
(Military Division)
(OLM)

Member of the
Legion of Merit
(Military Division)
(MLM)

Military Forces'
Commendation
(Operational)
(MFC Op)

Military Forces'
Commendation
(Non-Operational)
(MFC Non-Op)

Most Excellent
Order of the British
Empire the Military
Division (BEM)

Silver Medal for
Valour
(Italy)

Croix de Guerre
(France)

Medaille Militaire
(France)

Silver Cross of
Rhodesia
(SCR)

Bronze Cross of
Rhodesia
(BCR)

The Defence Cross
for Distinguished
Service
(DCD)

Defence Force
Medal for
Meritorious Service
(DMM)

Appendix IV

Colours and Uniforms

Colours

In 1951, the commander of Southern Rhodesia's defence forces suggested to the Regiment that the time may be right to apply for its own colours. After the first design was not accepted on the basis that it did not conform to the rules, the inspector general of colours was asked to come up with a suitable design, but with the proviso that, because the regiment transcended many nationalities, no patron saint cross be incorporated.

Her Majesty Queen Elizabeth II approved the final design, a bottle green flag carrying the regimental badge in colour, within a garter inscribed 'The Rhodesian African Rifles', surrounded by a wreath and surmounted by the Crown.

On 12 July 1953, a crowd of 10,000 witnessed Her Majesty Queen Elizabeth, the Queen Mother, present the Regiment with the Queen's Colours. Following the Royal Salute, Commanding Officer Lieutenant-Colonel Kim Rule, OBE, reported to Her Majesty that fifteen officers, fourteen British warrant officers and NCOs, and 535 African ranks were present on parade.

Battle Honours

The Federal Government Gazette 492/47 carried the decision by the War Office Board to award the following Battle Honours to the 1st Battalion, The Rhodesian African Rifles:

"Burma 1944-45"
"Arakan Beaches"
"Taungup"

In November 1962, after considerable representation to the governor-general by the then Regimental Association president, Colonel GE Wells OBE, ED, Her Majesty's Government awarded the Regiment the following additional Battle Honours earned by its predecessor, the Rhodesia Native Regiment:

"The Great War"
"East Africa 1916–18"

Regimental Badges

Rhodesian African Rifles

Initially, the only 'badge' worn by the newly formed regiment was a diamond-shaped piece of black cloth – a flash – displayed on the upturned brim of a slouch hat. The final iconic design featured a Zulu assegai crossed with a Shona digging spear, over an amaNdebele war shield. In the centre is an upright African club, called a *knobkerrie*. Below is a scroll carrying the title Rhodesian African Rifles. The badge came into official use in August 1940.

RAR HAT BADGES

Hat badge
Made by Firmin London 1940s - 1960s
Large font stamp on reverse

Officers hat badge
Hallmarked silver 1940s - 1960s

Hat badge
Flat back made by Matthews Rhodesia
1960s - on

Hat badge
Made by Firmin London 1940s - 1960s
Small font stamp on reverse

Cammo cap badge
1st Bn - 1970s

Cammo cap badge
1960s - 1970s

Cammo cap badge
2nd Bn - 1970s

Other Ranks hat badge
Made by Reuteler Rhodesia
1970s - 1980

Officers beret and collar badge
Hallmarked silver
Vertical lugs
1940s - 1960s

Officers beret and collar badge
Hallmarked silver
Horizontal lugs
1940s - 1960s

Cammo cap badge
2nd Bn - 1979

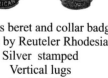 © DUDLEY WALL - 2013

Other Ranks collar badge
Made by Reuteler Rhodesia
1970s - 1980

Officers beret and collar badge
Made by Reuteler Rhodesia
Silver stamped
Vertical lugs
1970s - 1980

Regimental Uniforms

RNR askari in drill order, 1916.

RNR officer in No. 1 dress, 1916.

RNR askari on ops, East Africa, 1917.

RNR BNCO on ops, East Africa, 1917.

RAR officer, working dress, SR, 1940.

RAR askari corporal, drill order, SR, 1941.

RAR askari in field marching order, 1944.

RAR askari in ops, Burma, 1945.

RAR askari in No. 1 dress, Malaya, 1957.

RAR askari Bren gunner on ops, Malaya, 1957.

RAR officer on ops, Malaya, 1957.

RAR officer in No. 1 dress, Malaya, 1957.

RAR officer in combat kit, Rhodesian bush war, 1970s.

RAR officer in No. 1 dress, 1975.

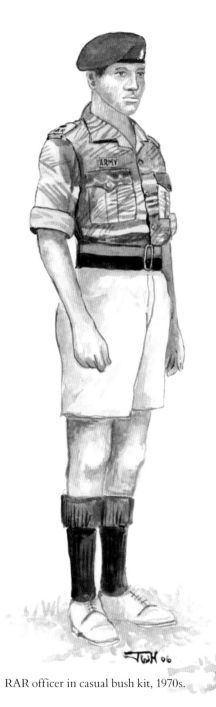

RAR officer in casual bush kit, 1970s.

RAR officer in sand dress, April 1981.

RAR MAG gunner in combat kit, Rhodesian bush war, 1970s.

RAR soldier in barrack dress, 1979.

RAR lance-corporal in No. 1 dress, 1975.

RAR paratrooper in jump kit,
Rhodesian bush war, 1970s.

The Regimental Mascot

The Regiment's first attempt at acquiring a mascot was the consideration of the fleet-footed zebra, but handling and training of such an animal proved very problematic. Thinking then moved to a donkey, but the very nature of the creature did not lend itself to that of military prowess. Finally, in May 1965, a young goat was presented to the regiment. Immediately christened 'Induna', the fast-learning mascot soon learned to kneel in salute at the command of 'Present Arms'. After many years of dedicated service, during which time he became as popular as the band which he headed, 'Induna' was succeeded by 'Private Tendai'.

Regimental Drum Skin

In September 1946, Field Marshal Bernard Montgomery of Alamein paid a brief visit to Rhodesia, and after inspecting the guard of honour, the indomitable veteran of many famous battles, paused by the bass drum of the band to sign his name on the drum skin. The concerned bandsman afterwards went to the bandmaster to express his consternation over the manner in which Monty had defaced his precious drum. Undeterred, however, the bandmaster carefully removed the drum skin and, mounting it in a hoop, presented it to the officers' mess.

It was thus that this item became an historic regimental icon, over the years having the signatures of many famous and well-known people inscribed on it. These include Her Majesty the Queen, the Duke of Edinburgh, the Prince of Wales, Louis Mountbatten of Burma, successive governors-general, Rhodesian presidents, Prime Minister Ian Smith, senior army officers, battalion commanding officers, and the last governor of Southern Rhodesia, Lord Christopher Soames.

Appendix V

Maps

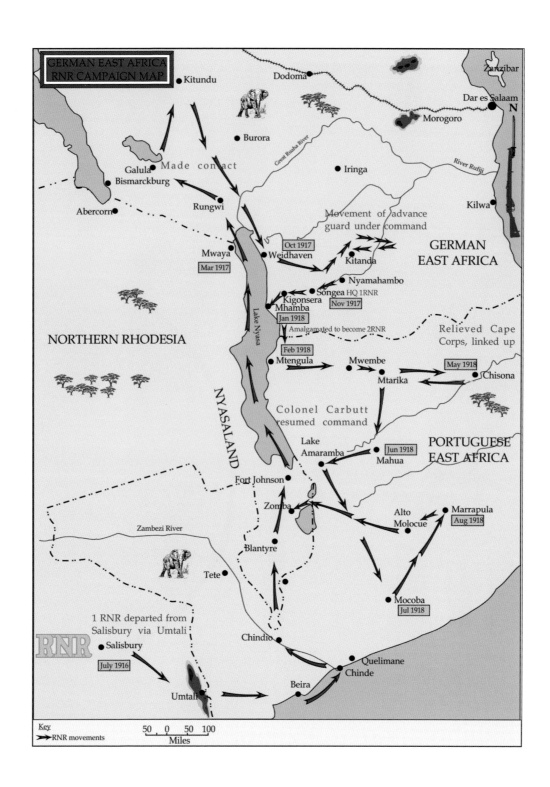

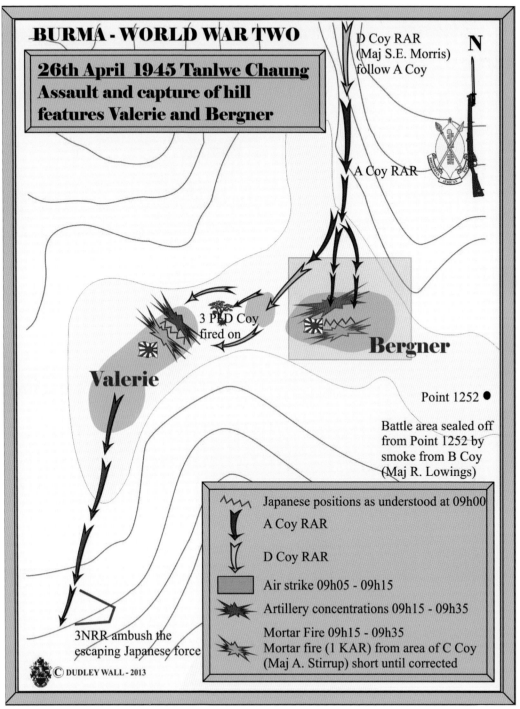

ROUTE OF ADVANCE OF THE RAR IN BURMA

N

INDIA

14th Army

Chittagong

Irrawaddy River

4 Corps

33rd Indian Corps

Mandalay

Moungdaw

12th Army

BURMA

15th Indian Corps

33rd Army

SIAM (THAILAND)

15th Army

Ramree

Taungup Pass

28th Army

Bay of Bengal

Rangoon

Movements of the RAR

© DUDLEY WALL - 2013

BURMA - WORLD WAR TWO

N

26th April 1945 Tanlwe Chaung
Assault and capture of hill features Valerie and Bergner

D Coy RAR (Maj S.E. Morris) follow A Coy

A Coy RAR

3 PLD Coy fired on

Bergner

Valerie

Point 1252 ●

Battle area sealed off from Point 1252 by smoke from B Coy (Maj R. Lowings)

Japanese positions as understood at 09h00

A Coy RAR

D Coy RAR

Air strike 09h05 - 09h15

Artillery concentrations 09h15 - 09h35

Mortar Fire 09h15 - 09h35
Mortar fire (1 KAR) from area of C Coy (Maj A. Stirrup) short until corrected

3NRR ambush the escaping Japanese force

© DUDLEY WALL - 2013

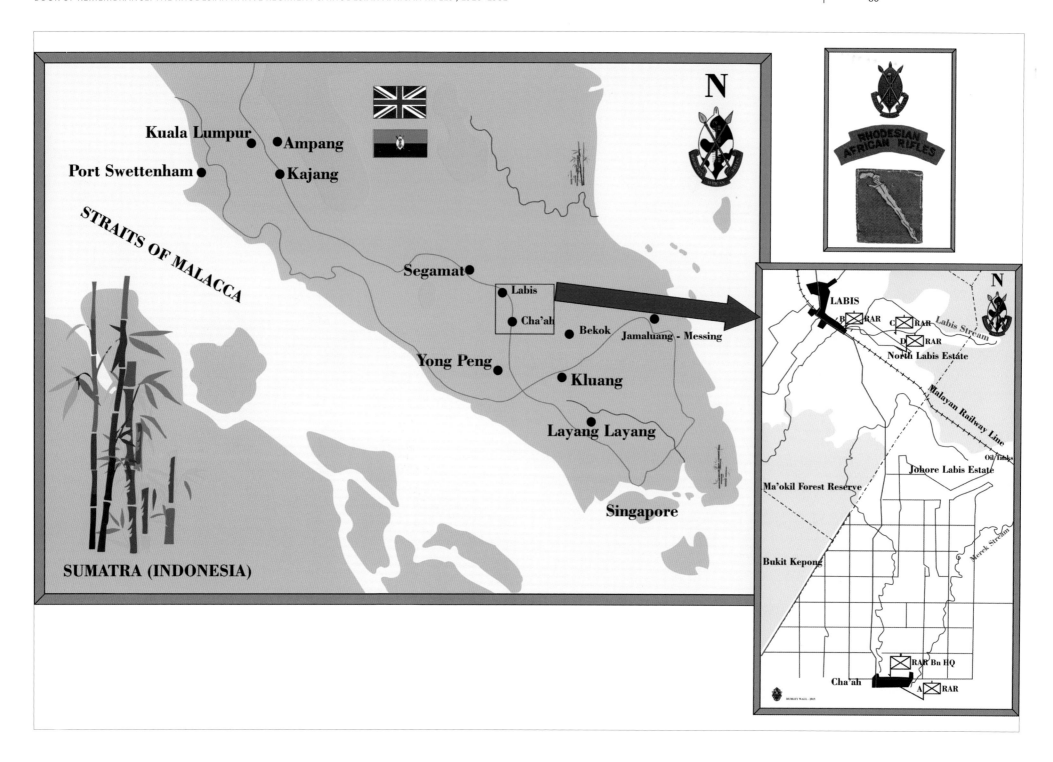

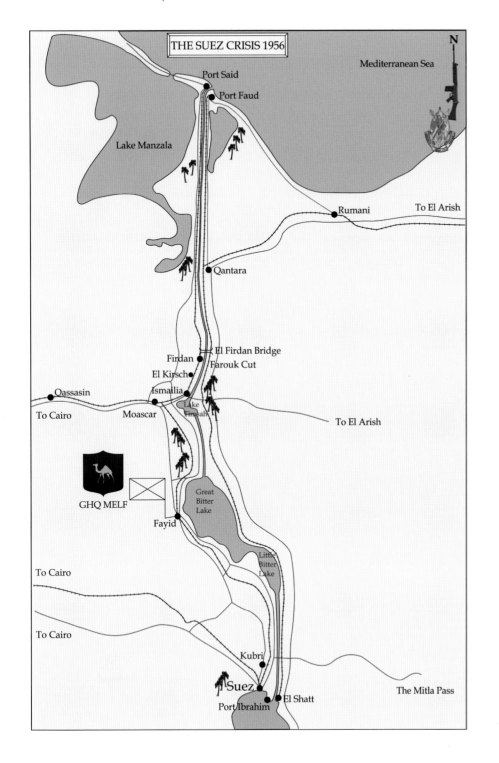

THE SUEZ CRISIS 1956

Mediterranean Sea

Port Said
Port Faud
Lake Manzala
Rumani — To El Arish
Qantara
El Firdan Bridge
Firdan
Farouk Cut
El Kirsch
Qassasin
Ismailia
To Cairo
Moascar
Lake Timsah
To El Arish
GHQ MELF
Great Bitter Lake
Fayid
Little Bitter Lake
To Cairo
To Cairo
Kubri
Suez
El Shatt
The Mitla Pass
Port Ibrahim

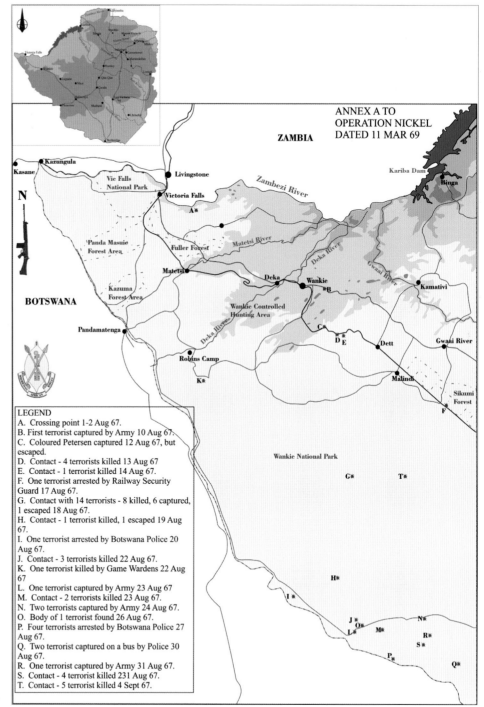

ANNEX A TO
OPERATION NICKEL
DATED 11 MAR 69

ZAMBIA
Kariba Dam
Binga
Kasane
Kazungula
Livingstone
Vic Falls National Park
Victoria Falls
Zambezi River
Panda Masuie Forest Area
Fuller Forest
Matetsi River
Deka River
Gwaai River
Matetsi
Deka
Wankie
Kamativi
BOTSWANA
Kazuma Forest Area
Wankie Controlled Hunting Area
Pandamatenga
Dett
Gwaai River
Robins Camp
Malindi
Sikumi Forest
Wankie National Park

LEGEND
A. Crossing point 1-2 Aug 67.
B. First terrorist captured by Army 10 Aug 67.
C. Coloured Petersen captured 12 Aug 67, but escaped.
D. Contact - 4 terrorists killed 13 Aug 67
E. Contact - 1 terrorist killed 14 Aug 67.
F. One terrorist arrested by Railway Security Guard 17 Aug 67.
G. Contact with 14 terrorists - 8 killed, 6 captured, 1 escaped 18 Aug 67.
H. Contact - 1 terrorist killed, 1 escaped 19 Aug 67.
I. One terrorist arrested by Botswana Police 20 Aug 67.
J. Contact - 3 terrorists killed 22 Aug 67.
K. One terrorist killed by Game Wardens 22 Aug 67
L. One terrorist captured by Army 23 Aug 67
M. Contact - 2 terrorists killed 23 Aug 67.
N. Two terrorists captured by Army 24 Aug 67.
O. Body of 1 terrorist found 26 Aug 67.
P. Four terrorists arrested by Botswana Police 27 Aug 67.
Q. Two terrorist captured on a bus by Police 30 Aug 67.
R. One terrorist captured by Army 31 Aug 67.
S. Contact - 4 terrorist killed 231 Aug 67.
T. Contact - 5 terrorist killed 4 Sept 67.

RAR Deployments

Rubatsiro Sector

Kanyemba

MOZAMBIQUE

Nehanda Sector

Zambezi River

Chaminuka Sector

2 Indep Coy

ZAMBIA

Kariba

FAF 2

FAF 3

Rushinga

Sipolilo Centenary

Op Hurricane Takawira Sector

Northern Front
Region 2

Sinoia

Mt Darwin

FAF 4

Mazoe River

Mrewa

Mtoko

FAF 5

Chitepo Sector

Op Splinter

Sanyati River

Salisbury

Goromonzi

Victoria Falls

Marandellas

3 Indep Coy

Inyanga Tangwena Sector

FAF 1

Wankie

Hartley

Op Thrasher

3 RAR

1 Indep Coy

Umtali

5 Indep Coy

4 Indep Coy

Op Grapple Que Que

FAF 8

Chipinga 6 Indep Coy

Lupane

FAF 6

Monomotapa Sector

Nkai

Gwelo

Sabi River

Op Tangent

Op Repulse

Northern Front
Region 1

1 RAR

Fort Victoria

Bulawayo

2 RAR

Musikavanhu Sector

Plumtree

Shabani

Kezi

Depot RAR

BOTSWANA

Nuanetsi River

Gwanda

Chiredzi

FAF 7

FAF 10

Sector 1

Op Repulse

Rutenga

Sector 2

Southern Front
Region 3

FAF 9

MOZAMBIQUE

Beitbridge Sector 3

SOUTH AFRICA

OPERATIONAL AREAS
1. Rhodesian areas in blue
2. ZIPRA areas in yellow
3. ZANLA areas in red
FAF 1 Forward Air Fields

© DUDLEY WALL - 2015